# 500

# Tips *for* Further *and* Continuing Education Lecturers

**500 Tips from Kogan Page**

# 500

## *Tips for Further and Continuing Education Lecturers*

DAVID ANDERSON,
SALLY BROWN AND PHIL RACE

**KOGAN
PAGE**

London • Stirling (USA)

First published in 1997

Kogan Page Limited
120 Pentonville Road
London N1 9JN
and
22883 Quicksilver Drive
Stirling, VA 20166, USA

British Library Cataloguing in Publication Data

A CIP record for this book is available from the British Library.

ISBN 0 7494 2411 7

Typeset by Jo Brereton, Primary Focus, Haslington, Cheshire
Printed and bound in the UK by Creative Print and Design (Wales), Ebbw Vale

# Contents

# Acknowledgements

The authors are very grateful to a number of colleagues who made useful comments on the draft versions of this book. Janice Gray and Rob Archer found most of our typographical errors, but also suggested a number of additional tips. Steve McDowell found even more errors, and also helped the authors avoid various repetitions, and encouraged them to make many of the suggestions more concisely and clearly. Colleagues at Gloscat provided the authors with fresh insights into the realities of being a further education lecturer in the late 1990s, and we are particularly grateful to Alma O'Boyle and Lyn Hurley for their suggestions. We are also indebted to John Hurley, Jo Foster and Lesley Bennetts for their insightful comments on our draft versions. John Storan and the participants on his new lecturers' programme at South Bank University added additional ideas to Chapter 1.

# Why This Book Now?

We have written this book for lecturers in further and continuing education colleges, and for those who work with them, manage them or train them. The primary purpose of this book is to provide practical suggestions, some of which will be immediately useful to college lecturers, and which will help them to gain increased professional satisfaction from their own work. At the same time, we hope that many of our suggestions will help to ensure that the learning experience of students in further education is enhanced and consolidated.

In further and continuing education, it is widely recognized that there has been a climate of rapid change for some time, with factors contributing to the pressure on staff including:

- the demand for growth at the same time as making efficiency savings;
- the publication of performance indicators for institutions, and the effects of this on funding and recruitment;
- continuing rapid changes in curriculum;
- the use of casual staff in colleges, with increased proportions of part-time teachers being drawn from commerce and industry;
- changes in funding arrangements;
- greater diversity of needs accompanying widening participation in further and continuing education;
- increased emphasis on lifelong learning; and
- the move towards colleges and institutions taking more responsibility for the assessment and enhancement of the quality of their own provision.

Combinations of factors such as those listed above constitute a formidable accumulation of challenges which stretch the skills of college managers, governors, and staff.

A report published in England in 1997 (FEFC, 1997) brings together a listing of some of the main challenges facing further and continuing education internationally as well as in the UK. Ten such challenges are listed below.

1   To develop and implement resource-based learning to accommodate a progressive reduction in 'taught' hours for typical students.

2   To recognize and accommodate the problems of achieving growth targets at a time when funding provision is becoming more diversified and less in quantity.

3   To improve college management information systems, so that reliable data on student recruitment, retention and achievements are available to inform quality assurance inspections and quality enhancement developments.

4   To update learning materials and resources, to keep pace with the revolution in information technology and its effect on the world of work for which students are being prepared.

5   To recognize and address the reality of a situation where the pace of change has contributed to unprecedentedly low staff morale in many areas of the sector.

6   To cater for the significant difficulties of part-time teachers, who often are unable to benefit adequately from staff development provision, and whose working life conditions are sometimes quite unsatisfactory.

7   To train college managers and governors to be better equipped to manage change.

8   To pay increasing attention to factors affecting student motivation, to combat tendencies for low attendance on college-based courses.

9   To address urgently the issue of student retention rates, where contributory factors to drop out include uneven tutorial support, insufficient pre-entry diagnosis and advice, and inadequate study-skills support for students.

10  To develop a robust self-critical culture in colleges, so that quality assurance procedures based on self-assessment are founded on a secure basis.

It is clearly not possible for individual staff members in further education to address each and every such challenge directly. However, through the suggestions in this book, we aim to assist further education staff to help themselves (and protect their sanity), by encouraging them to find ways of making their everyday working lives more successful, more efficient and less stressful. The cumulative effect of this should have significant impact on the ability of colleges to address challenges such as those listed above.

This book is designed to be used in several different ways.

• A personal companion to new teachers entering the profession, providing a source of tried-and-tested ideas and advice, which individuals can adapt to their own circumstances.

• Affirmation for all the experienced and dedicated further education teachers whose practice already accommodates and exceeds the suggestions offered in the book, with the hope that they too will find at least some ideas which spark off further creativity and initiatives in their work.

- A resource for course teams, to identify an agenda for development, and help towards planning new strategies, and implementing new procedures where necessary.

- A staff development tool, providing ideas for discussion and elaboration to fuel staff development training programmes.

- A college managers' resource, to help with the realistic design of pro-grammes of change.

The authors welcome the emerging climate in colleges in the UK and elsewhere that increasingly blurs the distinction between what they used to call 'academic' and 'support' staff. We know of colleges where all staff are employed on a single 'spine'. Our book is intended to help *all* staff in colleges, however their current job title describes them.

You may notice that there are well over 600 hundred suggestions in our book, and will therefore forgive us for repeating similar messages sometimes when a particular idea is relevant to more than one area. Also, we have sometimes given basic suggestions in a section, then elaborated on them in other parts of the book. We have usually chosen not to cross-reference our suggestions, to help each set of suggestions to be more-or-less self-explanatory and complete in itself.

We hope that readers of this book will feel pride and celebrate the fact that they will have already exceeded many of the suggestions we offer in this book. Equally, we hope that readers just starting out on any of the agendas covered by this book will not feel that the scale of our suggestions is intimidating, and will find suitable starting points among our tips. We welcome suggestions from readers for further or better tips and will be delighted to acknowledge these in our next edition; please send us your comments.

*David Anderson, Sally Brown and Phil Race, 1997*

# Chapter 1  Curriculum Matters

The nature of the curriculum delivered in further and continuing education settings has changed at an unprecedented rate in the last few years. For new lecturers, finding out how the curriculum works is a major task, and for experienced lecturers it is almost as hard to keep up with the changes.

We begin this chapter looking at a range of teaching–learning methodologies. This is, we believe, the most appropriate place to start this book as a whole, as choice of teaching–learning methods is usually the most important starting place in working out exactly how to go about developing how we implement the delivery of the curriculum to optimize student learning.

This leads us on to explore learning processes. Much has been written about learning styles, and students' approaches to studying (not to mention teachers' approaches to teaching). We prefer, however, to share with you some practical, jargon-free and straightforward ideas about the best ways to view student learning, so that teaching practices and learning situations can be tuned into this most important dimension.

Having paid some attention to *how* students learn, the next issue to tackle is *what* they should be learning. Expressing syllabus content in terms of behavioural objectives was a major step towards clarifying to staff and students alike the intentions surrounding each piece of the curriculum. More recently, syllabus content is expressed in terms of intended learning outcomes, with performance criteria describing to both staff and students the standards they need to reach to demonstrate their achievement of the intended outcomes. Evidence descriptors are used to show students the extent and depth of the evidence that they will need to furnish so as to demonstrate their performance against the performance criteria.

Next we move to the planning of a new teaching–learning programme. In a book of this style, we can only try to alert you to the principal issues that need to be considered in designing a new programme, but many later parts of the book also relate to this task, particularly Chapter 4 on assessment.

This chapter continues with an extended set of suggestions on developing students' key skills. In further education in the UK in particular, much attention has been given to the importance of students developing transferable life skills, and the necessity for college-based programmes to achieve such development through each part of the subject-based curriculum rather than as an add-on or afterthought. We hope that our suggestions on key skills will help colleagues to increase their ability to see where a piece of work for students relates to the subject centrally involved, as well as furnishing students with useful evidence for the key skills agenda.

We end this chapter with some suggestions on how to go about adjusting to curriculum change. It is probable that the way the curriculum is expressed, delivered and assessed will continue to change and develop, hopefully for the better. The skills of being able to accommodate these changes are an important part of the survival kit of the further or continuing education lecturer.

# 1

# Thinking about teaching–learning methodologies

Before choosing any particular teaching–learning activity for the delivery of a particular part of the curriculum, you will find it useful to explore some of the possibilities that can be chosen. Where alternative methods of delivery are being planned, the range of options given below provides a starting point towards working out which may be the most appropriate to consider. In principle, it should be possible to use several different alternative methodologies for any element of the curriculum, but each alternative will have its own advantages and drawbacks, both economically and pedagogically.

1   **Full-time taught courses, lecture-based.** Employers sometimes want their personnel to be trained or updated using such a strategy, often because this is how they themselves were taught. Such courses may work out more expensive than they expect, when taking into account the time off the job, travelling expenses to attend college, and the cost of the teaching staff involved. Apart from staffing, they require little in the way of resources or facilities. Start and finish dates for courses are likely to be inflexible, and the curriculum and assessment package delivered may only be fine-tuned to the actual needs of the individual students involved at a considerable additional cost. However, such courses have the benefits associated with social interaction between students, and between tutors and students.

2   **Part-time taught courses.** They share many of the above characteristics, but involve less time off the job for people who are already employed while retaining the advantage of face-to-face contact with tutors, and a limited opportunity for social interaction among students.

3   **Work-based training programmes.** These are essentially teaching–learning strategies that involve learners being trained while working at their normal employer's location, or having placements arranged in a

suitable employment location for a given period of time. The relevance of the content of the training to the learners' overall needs is more easily guaranteed, but the time and effort of supervising and assessing such training can be considerable. With National Vocational Qualifications they are usually a requirement. There can also be elements required of learners that cannot be directly measured in this way: the so-called underpinning knowledge and understanding.

4    **Realistic work environments.** This term is often used for training available at a college in a created work environment such as a hairdressing salon, café, travel agency or motor repair shop. Such training may be easier to arrange, oversee and assess than work-based training programmes, but the range of provision may be more limited. Underpinning knowledge and understanding may be more effectively addressed by the coexistence of other teaching–learning methodologies within the college.

5    **Distance learning programmes.** These cover situations where learners work through specifically designed self-study materials (often print-based) on their own, at a distance from the college, at times and places of their own choosing, and at their own pace. The institution provides a mark and comment service, often accompanied by some tutorial support and counselling. The assessment of such learning may have to be arranged at specific times, imposing some restrictions on the timing and pace of the learning. There may be only occasional direct contact with the institution. The collective shared experience associated with class-based methods does not exist and this individualized approach may not be attractive to learners or tutors.

6    **Resource-based learning.** This includes learning workshops, open access and drop-in centres where the institution offers tuition, counselling and learning support, plus access to materials and equipment. The materials may be print-based, computer-based or multimedia in nature, and there will be opportunities for group and individual contact with tutors, as well as access to college-based assessment provision. This methodology often requires a considerable initial investment in providing appropriate accommodation, equipment and support staff. Materials may not need the same degree of specific development as for distance learning programmes.

7    **Online learning.** This methodology includes computer-based learning, which may be college-based or done using networked computer facilities at the learners' workplace locations. Tutorial support and learning materials are networked to the computer terminals where learners study, and their study times can be varied to suit their individual requirements. Virtual or real-time group working is also possible, along with one-to-one tutor contact.

8    **Collaborative learning.** This methodology is used when it is intended that learners work together in small groups for significant parts of their learning. It can be arranged as a college-based process, or for learners to undertake in their workplace or in the actual situations they are learning about.

9    **Independent study pathways.** These are considered to be particular elements of the curriculum which individual learners are able to choose or adapt to their particular needs or requirements. They may involve using print-based or computer-based learning resource materials, on or off the college campus. By definition they are individualized but will normally involve tutor contact and support.

10   **Mixed mode delivery.** As the term implies, this means a combination of the different teaching–learning strategies already listed above, with perhaps some college-based teaching, some resource-based and some work-based learning. In reality you will find some element of mixed mode delivery in many courses.

# 2

# Exploring learning processes

One of the most important factors that predetermines success in learning is confidence. We need to give our learners every chance to develop this confidence, and one of the best ways of helping them to do this is to enable them to gain greater control over the processes they apply during their learning. Much of the content of this book addresses learning processes in various contexts, so we start here with just some key points, and return to expand on many of them in later parts of the book. The following suggestions should help you to show learners how they can adjust their approaches to learning to optimize their success.

1   **Learners need motivation.** They need to want to learn things. If they already want to learn, it is described as intrinsic motivation. They may need to be helped to increase their motivation by showing them what the benefits are for them flowing from the achievement of their intended learning outcomes. This generates extrinsic motivation. When possible, make learning fun, interesting and rewarding, and try to turn extrinsic into intrinsic motivation. Don't mistake lack of confidence for lack of motivation.

2   **Learning-by-doing is important.** Most learning happens when learners practise things, have a go, and learn by making mistakes and finding out why. Learners need to be given early opportunities to try out and apply new things that they have been introduced to. Care needs to be taken to ensure that learning-by-doing is focused on practising *useful* things, and not just anything to keep learners busy!

3   **Feedback to learners is essential.** They need to find out how their learning is actually going. They may feel that they have understood something, but cannot be certain until they find out whether they are handling it successfully. Feedback from tutors is very useful, but tutors can also facilitate learners getting feedback from each other, and from various kinds of learning resource materials. Remember that feedback must be timely for it to be of use to the learner. Any significant delay in the return of an assessed piece of written work usually causes gloom and distress.

4 **Needing to learn something can be almost as productive as wanting to learn it.** When learners know *why* something will be useful to them, even if they find it difficult, they are more likely to maintain their efforts until they have succeeded.

5 **Learners need to make sense of what they are learning.** It is of little value learning things by rote, or being able to do things without knowing why or how. Getting learners to think about how their learning is happening is one step towards helping them to develop a sense of ownership of their progress.

6 **Learning is not just a matter of storing up further knowledge.** Successful learning is about being able to apply what has been learned, not just to familiar situations but also to new contexts. It is essential to keep in mind the need to help students to learn in both sequential and holistic ways, and to look for ways to help them employ all of their senses to optimize their learning.

7 **Learners take cues about how they are expected to learn from the ways in which we teach them.** If we simply concentrate on supplying them with information, it is likely that they will simply try to store it. If we structure our teaching so that they are practising, applying, extending, comparing, contrasting, evaluating (using higher-level processes), they are likely to see these processes as central to the ways they should be learning.

8 **Learning is linked strongly to assessment.** Students are often quite strategic in structuring their learning so as to be able to do the best they can in the contexts in which their learning is to be assessed. Assessment formats and instruments can be used to help learners to structure their learning effectively, as well as to give them appropriate timescales within which to organize their learning.

9 **Learning is not just an independent activity.** While much can be learned by learners working on their own, with handouts, books and learning resource materials, they can also learn a great deal by talking to each other, and attempting tasks and activities jointly.

10 **Becoming better at learning is important.** The most important learning outcomes of being a student are not the syllabus-based, course specific ones, but are the outcomes relating to becoming better able to learn new skills and competences. Learning skills are among the most important of the transferable life skills. The course content can be regarded as a vehicle through which these important skills are developed.

# 3

# Expressing learning outcomes

For many lecturers in further education, syllabus content will already be expressed in competence framework terms, including learning outcomes, performance criteria and range statements. However, many such frameworks have been written primarily for awarding bodies, bureaucrats and lecturers rather than in language that students themselves can understand and make use of. The following suggestions may help you to extend the benefits of expressing and clarifying learning outcomes to your students, and to the assessment schemes you devise to assess their achievements.

1   **Work out exactly what you want students to be able to do by the end of a defined learning element.** You may have been trained to do this as part of the process of making lesson plans, and you may be working with syllabus content that is already expressed in terms of learning outcomes or objectives. Nevertheless, it is often worth thinking again about the exact intentions, and working out how these connect together for different parts of students' learning.

2   **Express learning outcomes in terms of actions.** Try to explain what lies behind phrases such as 'will be able to understand' or 'will know'. The words you choose to describe learning outcomes should enable students themselves to tell exactly what the intentions are.

3   **Work out the associated evidence.** Think about how students will be required to demonstrate their achievement of the learning outcomes in terms of what they will be able to use to show that they have succeeded.

4   **Don't overdo the evidence!** There is wide agreement that students tend to be over-assessed, and that they are required to produce too much evidence to demonstrate each particular element of competence. It is better to choose the most appropriate kinds of evidence carefully, than to list all the possible kinds of evidence that could relate to each learning outcome.

5    **Work out performance criteria.** Decide how students' actions and evidence can be judged and assessed. Formulate these criteria in words that can be understood by students themselves, rather than phrasing them in the types of academic jargon that occurs too often in published syllabus specifications or competence-based frameworks.

6    **Work out descriptions to help students see how much, and what kinds of evidence they need.** These are sometimes called 'range statements', and the intention is to help students know what they need to do in terms of extent and standards to meet performance criteria, and to demonstrate that they have achieved learning outcomes.

7    **Provide students with the whole picture.** Put the student-centred language descriptions of learning outcomes, performance criteria and range indicators into student handbooks, or short self-contained leaflets to give to students at the beginning of the course. Where the contents are based on published specifications (such as those for GNVQ), include the original specifications as an appendix, so that students can see the source of the material. This leaflet or handbook component should serve students as a map enabling them to navigate their own way through the learning programme as they study.

8    **Ensure that students do not feel swamped by the enormity of the whole picture.** While it is important to provide the picture, there is a danger that it can appear very daunting, especially at the beginning of a course. Students need to be guided carefully in ways that allow them to feel confident that they will be able to succeed a step at a time.

9    **Where possible, provide alternatives.** Rather than requiring students to demonstrate their achievement of each part of the competence framework separately, look for tasks that embrace a number of different learning outcomes and performance criteria at the same time, so that students' work, and your assessment of it, will not go into overload.

10   **Select learning outcomes, performance criteria and so on, and relate them to individual class sessions.** Relate them similarly to each student assignment, and each learning task. Students need to know how each thing they are doing fits into the overall picture of their course or module.

11   **Work out your assessment breakdown.** Decide how you are going to structure the assessment of each important learning outcome, linking the assessment to the performance criteria you have formulated. Ensure that the scope and scale of the assessment are described accurately by the range indicators you have written.

12   **Ensure that your students are clear about what is expected of them.**
     Check that they know what you are looking for in terms of assessment-
     related evidence. Where possible, allow individual negotiation of what
     can count as appropriate evidence.

# 4

# Planning a new programme

Designing a new area of curriculum delivery is an exciting but complex task, requiring the integration of a whole range of interdependent elements. The following set of tips is designed to help you do so in a systematic way and are in sequence. These are most likely to be of use to you if you are (or will be) in the role of course leader for the new programme.

1   **Identify the market for your programme.** Few new programmes these days are offered to a captive, predetermined market of potential students. You will need, therefore, to have good evidence of a real demand for *your* programme. You will need to identify the competition – other bodies offering a similar programme. Can you show that either the market is sufficiently large or that you can offer something very different to attract a sufficient number of students? Your college will probably require you to show how your programme will sit within the existing course portfolio.

2   **Clarify the rationale for the new programme.** You need to be sure of your reasons for its particular flavour and its ultimate viability. Can you run it with the human and physical resources available? Can you provide for a sufficiently large number of students, at a price they can afford? Specifically consider: the unique characteristics of the client group it is aimed at; the programme's aims, intended learning outcomes; and the qualification or accreditation that it will lead to.

3   **Clarify how it will be resourced.** This is a daunting process if it is your first time, and we advise you to gather know-how from other colleagues in your institution who have already planned and implemented a new programme. That said, here are some of the things you will need to address. Given your client group and the qualification outcomes (if any), you now need to determine whether you can attract funding from government or other agencies, in whole or in part. Some advanced courses can be designated so that would-be students will have their fees and expenses paid. A large number of courses in England are supported either by the Further Education Funding Council (FEFC) or Higher Education

Funding Council for England (HEFCE). Others are sponsored by Training and Enterprise Councils (TECs), employers or local government. If your programme meets none of these agencies' criteria, will your potential students have to pay for the full costs of their study? Do you have evidence that there are sufficient numbers who could afford the full cost, or are there other ways to support them? In all cases, you'll need to prepare a financial and resource budget for the new programme.

4   **Decide on a time frame.** Curriculum design is a complex and time-consuming process. Mistakes are made if the process is rushed. If a programme is to be designed from scratch, sufficient time should be allowed to negotiate and incorporate internal as well as external quality assurance processes. Time is also needed to market the course effectively. Be realistic about a start date.

5   **Expect to become involved in the recruitment of students.** It is often found, particularly with new programmes, that students receive inappropriate guidance and advice, and can end up taking a course for which they are not suited. A useful part of planning a new programme is to look at how students will be guided before they enrol, and the kinds of follow-up support they are most likely to need after enrolment. Such guidance has been found to be an essential factor in ensuring that students do not drop out of new programmes.

6   **Determine learning outcomes.** If these already exist in a suitably specified format, they provide your start point. This will be the case, for example, if your new programme is designed to be accredited under the National Vocational Qualifications scheme. Otherwise, you will need to design learning outcomes, based on the programme rationale and its target client group, that are specific, measurable, achievable, realistic and time-constrained (SMART).

7   **Decide on how the outcomes are to be addressed.** It can be helpful when planning the delivery of most learning outcomes to use the specific terminology of the UK's vocational qualification movement: 'performance criteria', 'evidence indicators' and 'range statements'. When expressed in simple, jargon-free language, you will find that both your students and colleagues will be clear about what is required of them. You will also find that the learning outcome will be redefined as manageable chunks of activity.

8   **Consider appropriate teaching and learning strategies.** You will need to decide to what extent you will use traditional teaching methods, resource-based learning and flexible learning pathways in the delivery of your programme. It is important to reflect the particular circumstances of your

client group and individual differences in learning style. Therefore, it is unlikely that you will want to use a single strategy. For every alternative there will be specific staff and resource implications.

9   **Think about who will deliver it.** You will probably need to assemble a course team to deliver the programme. It is not a good idea to design a programme that is dependent on the particular qualifications or expertise of individual staff members. Typically they will leave or drop out in due course. This requires you to identify a pool of appropriate staff to which you can turn. It is a good idea, therefore, to assemble a collection of CVs of all likely staff you come across.

10  **Think carefully about the resources you will need to run the programme effectively.** These will include teaching staff, support staff, library and information technology resources. You may also need to budget for laboratory, workshop or studio facilities, specialized equipment, printing and photocopying. Do not assume that college resources and facilities will be automatically available to you just because the programme is approved.

11  **Consider what staff development the team may need to deliver the programme effectively.** There will be training needs associated with any new programme, such as using unfamiliar delivery methods, content updating or simply teambuilding.

12  **Decide how the learning outcomes will be assessed.** It is common to express the content of a programme in terms of what students will be able to do or know. Good decisions on how best to assess whether the specified learning outcomes have been achieved are crucial. There is a real danger of assessing only some of the learning outcomes and then only partially. For this reason, put assessment (and quality assurance) at the top of your list of things to get right.

13  **Plan carefully for the internal and external validation processes that will be required.** If you have yet to experience a validation event, talk to someone who has. If practical, involve such a person in your own preparations for the event, perhaps even to do a dry run with you. Scrutinize your own college's internal validation processes and ensure that you complete all the required paperwork in good time. If you are working with a higher education partner or a professional body you will also need to be fully acquainted with their processes. External accreditation will require further form filling and scrutiny of the relevant examining and validating body.

14   **Think about the values that underpin your programme.** For example, your underpinning philosophies about how students learn need to be explicit, agreed and shared by the course team. Your programme will need to meet your college's equal opportunities requirements in such terms as access and provision for special needs.

15   **Plan into the structure of the programme a process of continuous quality review and improvement.** It is critical that you look at how you will monitor the success of your programme. This will include student and sponsor satisfaction, peer review, retention and completion rates, and assessment reliability. The means for disseminating and using such data need to be considered, such as the creation and operation of a programme management committee with student and sponsor representation.

# 5

# Developing students' key skills

There has been a lot of attention in recent years to the development of central or transferable skills in students, and to the use of the subject-based curriculum as a vehicle for this development. The UK Dearing Further Education Review (1996) stressed that the students aged 16–19 needed to develop their six 'key skills' (communication, working with others, improving their own learning and performance, problem solving, information technology and the application of number) within the context of their main course programmes. The Further Education Development Agency (FEDA) project on 'Core Skills Across the Curriculum' also highlighted this philosophy, and indicated how evidence of the demonstration of such skills could be recorded from students' achievements and experiences from a programme of study. We offer the following suggestions to help you implement students' development of these skills.

1    **Become as aware as possible of the links between each of the key skills and your own particular curriculum areas.** In practice, there is not much that students can do without using these skills in one way or another. Help students to recognize this and to collect evidence.

2    **Link key skills to each other.** For instance, the task of undertaking a survey can address many of the six key skills, particularly communication, application of number and information technology elements.

3    **Treat key skills holistically.** Try not to set up separate activities to address each performance criterion or element. For instance, the three 'application of number' elements make up a process – do not try to separate them.

4    **Help to ensure that evidence resulting from students' work serves a dual purpose.** It is important not to design artificial tasks that become additional hoops for students to jump through, relating to their accumulation of evidence covering the key skills. If the agenda of producing key skills evidence is not duly built in to the whole of the curriculum, it reverts to 'general studies' and the importance is

undermined. It is usually possible to adjust subject-specific tasks and activities so that students produce appropriate key skills evidence concurrently with their discipline-specific work.

5  **Liaise with colleagues to ensure that students are not required to cover the same ground too often.** If different areas of the curriculum require students to demonstrate evidence of the same key skills, you should ensure that they are not doing the same sort of activity too often. It is useful to establish which key skills are most directly associated with each individual subject or topic, and then to look for ways of addressing any of the key skills that are still 'missed' in the overall picture of students' work. Also, use their own specialist expertise to help you devise or fine-tune assignments.

6  **Consider using learning agreements to address key skills evidence.** This can have the benefit of giving students a sense of ownership of the ways that they individually go about accumulating their evidence of key skills development, and can help to provide an 'added value' ethos, rather than a 'minimum competencies' situation. The evidence derived from learning agreements can be vital in allowing students to demonstrate key skills relating to developing their own learning.

7  **Peer-assessment increases understanding in learners.** Get groups of learners to discuss and critique each other's evidence, and the performance criteria. You will find this works particularly well for the key skill of communication.

8  **Introduce your students to the specific key skills elements at the point of need.** For example, doing spreadsheets with your students in October, when they do not need to use those skills until they reach a specific finance and administration unit in February, does not make for effective learning.

9  **The key skills jargon is off-putting for students, as is the thought that it is maths and English yet again.** Talk positively about key skills as often as you can, and show students that when you strip the jargon and technical language away, they are useful skills. If *you* find the jargon difficult, find an appropriate colleague to talk you through the specifications.

10  **Collect examples of real life key skills.** Use anecdotal evidence to show learners the real relevance of a particular key skill. For example, the trainee hairdresser (who has to work out how much dye solution to make up for a third of a head of hair) needs to have appropriate number skills.

11    **Start the students off with a broad brush key skills assignment.** Design an initial activity that offers lots of key skills scope and gets learners used to identifying and recording key skills from the start.

12    **Emphasize each instance of application of number.** Ensure that any calculations that students do in class sessions or in set assignments allow their numerical work to constitute evidence in its own right to demonstrate this skill. It is useful to ensure that calculations are suitably diverse in nature, and meet the appropriate level.

13    **Highlight effective communication.** Getting evidence relating to written communication skills is relatively straightforward, and can be incorporated into most areas of the curriculum. Evidence of oral communication skills can be built into many parts of the curriculum in most subject areas, such as those associated with individual student or group presentations. Such evidence often arises from activities that represent good opportunities for learning, and for students to gain feedback not only from their lecturers but from each other.

14    **Make good use of information technology.** The growth in the use of computer-based learning resource materials enables students to gather evidence of their use of information technology, and to do so in the context of their subject-based studies, rather than having to undertake additional tasks to accumulate this type of evidence. When students are also using information technology for communication, such as e-mail, they can also use this to add to evidence of their communications skills. Further use of information technology may involve students' activities with the Internet, and most students will use spreadsheets or desktop publishing packages in the context of their coursework or classwork.

15    **Promote the benefits of improving learning and performance.** This key skill area may require further planning, even though most things students do involve such improvement. The important step is to ensure that students collect evidence that relates to them reflecting about *how* they learn things, and *how* they think about their own performance in the various tasks and activities that they undertake in the course of their studies. The use of learning agreements is a productive source for this kind of development.

16    **Strike a realistic balance between *improving* skills and *measuring* them.** When the evidence that students produce does not match up to performance criteria, students need opportunities for further practice, and may need to revisit some areas of their work before being assessed.

17 **Show the value of working with others.** This key skill is highly valued by employers, yet too often education programmes tend to measure students' individual work rather than their collaborative work. While it is sometimes difficult to establish how to assess collaborative work fairly, it remains very useful to set students collaborative tasks. It is productive to build into the assessment, elements that involve students themselves reflecting on how well (or how badly) the collaboration worked in practice.

18 **Provide opportunities for problem solving.** In some areas of the curriculum there is little difficulty in finding tasks and exercises where students can develop and demonstrate their problem solving skills. Case studies can be particularly useful to allow problem solving skills to be developed and demonstrated in situations that these students may expect to encounter in future employment.

19 **With competence-based schemes, start by looking at the range and evidence indicators, not the performance criteria.** With key skills programmes within the British General and National Vocational Qualification schemes, you will need to plan your students' activities and assignments from statements. Use the performance criteria as assessment tools (not as planning ones).

20 **With competence-based schemes, involve work experience providers (employers) in supplying witness statements**. Many of the difficult parts of the range statement requirements can only be addressed in live, work experience contexts. Your employer partners will need careful briefing and support.

21 **Put yourself through the process.** Do the key skills programme at one level above that which your students will have to do. This will help you understand the units and the assessment process more quickly than anything else.

*The authors are pleased to acknowledge the help of Judith Woodlock, Learning Support Manager, Gloscat in writing this section*

# 6

# Adjusting to curriculum changes

The pace of curriculum change seems to accelerate, and can become a significant contributory factor to work-related stress and overload. Many colleagues find themselves in situations where curriculum change is very much a 'top-down' process, and find it difficult to feel a healthy sense of ownership of the changes taking place. Nevertheless, there are usually good reasons behind curriculum changes, and it is important not to allow the problems of implementing change to blind one to the benefits which may be made possible as a result. The following suggestions may help you to confront the pressures you could be feeling from such changes.

1   **Don't overestimate the pace of curriculum changes.** When new syllabus specifications, performance criteria and assessment procedures come into being, it is natural to feel that everything is changing far too fast. However, in practice this rarely means that the whole of your work with students is meant to change at a stroke. It is more usual for much of the teaching and learning to change quite slowly, even when the systems within which these processes take place are radically redesigned.

2   **Be positive about changes.** There is usually at least one good reason behind any major change, and changes are opportunities to realize new benefits, both for your students and for yourself. It often takes far less energy simply to get on and accommodate the changes than to resist them and defend previous practices.

3   **Build on to changes.** Changes in syllabus specifications can provide you with opportunities to focus on the processes and content of your students' learning, and how they will be assessed. Such changes can give you the chance to abandon 'dead' parts of the curriculum, and to tune in to the things that your students will really need in the future.

4    **Use any opportunities to rethink the intended learning outcomes for your students.** It can be useful to adjust how these are expressed and communicated to students, to give them a firmer picture of exactly what they are intended to become able to do.

5    **Use all opportunities to adjust assessment processes.** For example, it may be possible to introduce new elements of self-assessment and peer-assessment, both of which can deepen students' learning experiences, and help them to tune in better to the nature of the assessment processes they encounter.

6    **Look for ways of helping students to get more feedback on their learning.** For example, the introduction of resource-based learning elements into the curriculum can be accompanied by a significant increase in the quantity and quality of the feedback that students can receive as they learn, especially if the learning resources are carefully chosen and adapted to meet their needs.

7    **Don't throw out things that worked well in the past.** It is useful to develop changes in practice on the strengths of the processes which are known to be trustworthy and effective.

8    **Accept that students themselves continue to change.** Students in further education have different aspirations and expectations than they did years ago. Who they are, and where they are coming from, have changed too. Students bring different strengths and weaknesses to their college work than in the past. Curriculum change can be harnessed as a natural way to adjust to the changing population of students.

9    **Identify appropriate learning resource materials.** Traditionally, publishers have been slowly reactive rather than proactive in bringing out relevant new materials. However, you will not be the only person clamouring for materials, and it is worth lobbying publishers who already produce materials relevant to your students, asking them to consider ideas that will be of even greater use. Keep talking about your needs to your college librarian and learning resources centre manager. New materials can be developed in-house. Relevant materials are increasingly found on the Internet, and can be downloaded and adapted.

10    **Don't forget that stasis is boring.** If there is too little change, boredom and inertia are significant causes of stress, and the stress caused by change may well be preferable.

# Chapter 2　Curriculum Delivery

This chapter continues the theme of working with the curriculum, but this time the focus is on practical ways of delivering it. We start by sharing some suggestions about one of the things that can cause the most significant problems when it goes wrong: classroom management. Most readers of this book will have developed their own strengths in this area, and will have learned (as have the authors) from numerous mistakes! We hope that our suggestions will provide at least some ideas to short-circuit the learning-by-mistakes pathway for readers.

We continue this chapter with an extended set of suggestions about 'learning in large groups' – or lectures as such occasions are described on our timetables and in our accounting procedures. We offer suggestions on how the large group session can be turned into an active learning experience for students, even when there are lots of them.

Next we provide some suggestions about getting students to work together. Evidence of such collaboration is useful for students to accumulate towards demonstrating their achievements relating to the key skills we discussed in the previous chapter. Here, we concentrate on the practicalities of helping students to work collaboratively. This leads us on naturally to some suggestions on student group projects. Project work is invaluable in that it allows us the flexibility to adapt nationally formulated curriculum specifications to be more realistic in local situations, and allows students greater flexibility in the ways that they demonstrate their achievement of the specified learning outcomes. We continue this thread by looking at how individual student projects can be designed to maximize the opportunity for students to demonstrate their own individual strengths, and to have the advantage of an increased feeling of ownership of the work that they are doing.

We move next to a set of suggestions on the broad issue of involving students in their own education, and its assessment. This paves the way for our more detailed suggestions under the heading 'Using learning agreements'.

We end the chapter with the important topic of 'Designing effective class assignments', which leads into the even more crucial area of assessing students in ways that are valid, fair and reliable. Assignments should promote students' learning rather than just measure snapshots of their achievement at particular points on their journeys through further education.

# 7

# Classroom management

A major component of any lecturer's work in further education colleges comes under this overall heading. Colleagues who have undertaken Certificate of Education courses will have had lesson planning ground into them. You may already have kept logs or records of class activities. Here we're interested in sharing some easily remembered techniques to maximize students' interest levels, and to minimize the opportunities for disruptive behaviour. Though we have some suggestions to offer, we recognize that there are many different ways to manage groups of students effectively, and that colleagues will each have their own tried-and-tested methods. Nonetheless, we hope that you may find something here to add to your own repertoire.

1   **Students work best when they know what they are trying to do.** It is important to articulate the specific intended learning outcomes of each particular session, and add your own explanation regarding why it is worthwhile for students to strive to achieve them.

2   **Part of your job is to warm up students' motivation.** If your class really wants to learn something, it will be an easy class to manage. The best way to help students develop a desire to learn something is to take enough time to explain to them what is in it for them, and why it will help them.

3   **Adjust the furniture.** If chairs, desks or tables are moveable, work out what configuration lends itself best to the purposes of your session. Getting all the students into a circle helps to ensure that everyone participates, and helps to prevent anyone opting out of discussions. Cafeteria-style arrangements are suitable for small-group work. It only takes a short time to get your students to move the furniture. Remember though that the next person to use the classroom may want it in its original configuration, so allow a few minutes to restore the previous arrangement.

4     **Keep your students busy.** Most of the problems that are encountered in classroom management are exacerbated if students are bored or idle. It is important, however, not just to keep them busy doing routine tasks such as copying things down as notes, but to give them interesting and challenging things to do, such as working out the consequences of an idea or an action.

5     **Ring the changes.** Attention spans are short – particularly for younger students – so remember to give them a variety of different things to do. Giving them a balanced mixture, alternating between individual tasks and group tasks, helps to provide them with a variety of stimuli and keep them learning. Use audio-visual aids to reinforce main points and to provide variety.

6     **Try to cater for mixed ability levels.** Students who are weak in basic skills can often become disruptive if the whole group is given tasks where they themselves need assistance. As far as possible, get to know the individuals in your class, so that you can address the particular needs of low-fliers before they cause any problems.

7     **Aim to get them all learning *in* the classroom.** This may indeed be your only chance. Do not assume that students will all go away from a class session and devote themselves to all the things you would like them to do to follow up, whatever was covered in the session. Try to aim for them to have a firm grip on the most important things you wish them to learn before they leave the session.

8     **Link classroom-based learning to self-managed learning.** With the widespread use of self-managed learning, it can be beneficial to use classroom-based sessions to help students to develop the approaches that will help when they are learning on their own.

9     **Use their names – and get them right!** Stephen may much prefer to be addressed as Steve, so find out what they would like you to call them. Students' levels of engagement in a session are increased if they feel that they are not just anonymous faces. Your knowledge of their names is valuable when occasions arise where you may need to chide someone who is being disruptive, or when you have the opportunity to praise someone who has done something well. Using Post-its as temporary name badges, or folded sheets of paper as place cards, are ways of getting to know at least some of their names quite quickly.

10   **Keep your temper.** This is sometimes easier said than done! However, losing control can be an irretrievable occurrence, and is worth striving to avoid. It is better to take any culprits aside in less-public settings than to risk a showdown with a whole class.

11   **Don't resort to any threats that you cannot deliver.** If it becomes necessary to adopt an authoritarian stance, even if only temporarily, it is important that you are seen to be able to handle fully the consequences that might arise.

12   **Don't duck awkward questions.** No one can be expected to have instant answers to every possible question. You will get more respect, when confronted by a question that you cannot answer then and there, to admit that 'This is a tough one; I'll find out for our next class'. Don't forget to do this.

# 8

# Learning in large groups

Lectures remain a fact of life for the majority of college students, despite the fact that they are a relatively inefficient way of promoting student learning, motivation and involvement. In the UK, new further education staff contracts with increased contact-hours, together with continual pressures to increase student numbers while reducing costs, guarantee a continued future for the lecture as a means of curriculum delivery. Also, lectures constitute one of the most 'public' forms of teaching, and therefore are high on the inspection and quality assurance agenda. These tips are designed to maximize the learning potential of lectures, and to remind you of ways that large-group sessions can pay real dividends to students.

1   **Make the most of opportunities when you have the whole group together.** There are useful benefits of whole-group shared experiences, especially for setting the scene in a new subject, and talking students through known problem areas. Use these as sessions to develop whole-group cohesion as well as to give briefings, provide introductions, introduce keynote speakers and to hold practical demonstrations.

2   **Make sure that lecture-type sessions are not 'transmit–receive' occasions.** Little is learned by learners just writing down what the lecturer says, or copying down information from screens or boards. There are more efficient ways of providing learners with the information they need for their learning, including the use of handout materials, textbooks and other learning resource materials.

3   **Make good use of the specific intended learning outcomes for each large group session.** Explaining these at the start of the session, or including them in handout materials, can help students to know exactly what they should be getting out of the session, serving as an agenda against which they can track their individual progress through the session.

4   **Work out some questions which the session will address.** Showing these questions as an overhead transparency at the beginning of the session is a way of helping learners to see the nature and scope of the specific learning outcomes they should be able to address progressively as the session proceeds.

5   **Learners can learn-by-doing in large groups.** Even in a lecture theatre, learners can be given tasks to do independently for a few minutes at a time, followed by a suitable debriefing, so that they can see whether they have been successful or not, and to find out why they may have made mistakes.

6   **Learners can get a lot of feedback from each other in large groups.** Getting students to work in small groups in a lecture environment can allow them to discuss and debate the relative merits of different options in multiple-choice tasks, or put things in order of importance, or brainstorm possible solutions to problems. After they have engaged with each other on such tasks, the lecturer can draw conclusions from some of the groups, and give expert witness feedback when needed.

7   **Large group sessions can be used to help learners make sense of things they have already learned.** It is valuable to make full use of the times when all learners are together to give them exercises to do so that they can check out whether they can still do the things covered in previous sessions. They can also check out how their learning successes or deficiencies compare with those of fellow learners.

8   **Large group sessions are useful when learners' attitudes need to be shaped or informed.** The elements of tone of voice, facial expression, body language and so on can be used by lecturers to bring greater clarity and direction to the attitude-forming shared experiences which help learners set their own scene for a topic or theme in a subject.

9   **Feedback can be drawn from learners in large group sessions.** Such sessions can be used to provide a useful barometer of how their learning is going. Learners can be asked to write on slips of paper (or Post-its) questions that they would like the lecturer to address at a future session.

10  **Large group sessions can be used to explain carefully the briefings for assessment tasks.** It is essential that all learners have a full, shared knowledge of exactly what is expected of them in such tasks, so that no one is disadvantaged by any differentials in their understanding of the performance criteria or assessment schemes associated with the tasks.

11   **Large group sessions can be used to go through the assessment criteria applied to learners' work.** This can be done by devising class sessions around the analysis of how past examples of students' work were assessed, as well as by going through in detail the way that assessment criteria were applied to work that the class members themselves have done.

12   **Record a sample of your large group sessions on video.** It is very salutary to see yourself working with a large group on video. Review the video to help you see your own strengths and weaknesses, and look for ways to improve your performance. Your keenest critic is likely to be yourself, so do not try to resolve every little habit or mannerism at once, just gradually tackle the ones that you think are most important. It may also be useful for a group of colleagues to look at each other's videos together, and offer each other constructive comments. This is excellent practice for inspection or other quality assessment procedures.

13   **Observe other people's large group sessions.** You can do this in your own college and also at external conferences and seminars. Watching other people helps you to learn, both from what others do well (which you might wish to emulate), to awful sessions where you resolve never to do anything similar in your own classes.

14   **Put energy and effort into making your large group sessions interesting and stimulating.** A well-paced lecture that has visual impact and in which ideas are clearly communicated can be a motivating shared experience for students. Become an expert in using overhead projectors and audio-visual equipment in imaginative ways.

15   **Remember that students have relatively short attention spans.** Make sure that you build into large group lectures a variety of activities for students, which might include writing, listening, looking, making notes, copying diagrams, undertaking small discussion tasks, asking questions, answering questions, giving feedback to you, solving problems, doing calculations, putting things in order of importance, and so on. At regular intervals, ask yourself 'and what are the students doing now?' If the answer is always the same throughout a lecture, you should be thinking how you can diversify further.

16   **Design a clear structure for each lecture.** Make links into previous material covered, and signpost what is to come next. Within the lecture itself, give students an idea of what you plan to cover in that particular lecture, and indicate throughout the session where what you are saying fits into the overall shape.

17    **Give your students some practice at note-making (rather than just note-taking).** Students learn very little just from copying out bits of what they see or hear, and may need quite a lot of help towards summarising, prioritising, and making their notes their own individual learning tools.

18    **Use large group sessions to identify and answer students' questions.** This can be much more effective, and fairer, than just attempting to answer their questions individually and privately. When one student asks a question in a large group session, there are often many other students who only then realize that they too need to hear the answer.

19    **Help the shy or retiring students to have equal opportunity to contribute.** Asking students in large groups to write questions, or ideas, on Post-its helps to ensure that the contributions you receive are not just from those students who are not afraid to ask in public. It can be comforting for students to preserve their anonymity in asking questions, as they are often afraid that their questions may be regarded as silly or trivial.

20    **Come to a timely conclusion.** A large-group session must not just fizzle out, but should come to a definite and robust ending. It is also important not to overrun. It is better to come to a good stopping place a few minutes early, than to end up rushing through something important right at the end of the session.

# 9

# Getting students to work together

Students often feel that they are competing with each other, and need considerable encouragement to relax such feelings and begin to work collaboratively effectively. The following suggestions should help to get your students started in productive group activities.

1   **Help students to understand why they need to be able to work together in groups.** Explain to students that there are real skills to be gained from group work tasks, and that the ability to contribute effectively to teams that they will develop is important to employers.

2   **Think about the different ways of forming groups.** These include forming groups randomly, using alphabetical lists, or forming groups on the basis of employment background, interest or ability, or allowing students to choose their own group compositions. Each method has its own advantages and drawbacks. The best compromise is to rotate group membership and ensure that students are not 'stuck' in the same group for too long, especially if the group dynamic is not working well.

3   **Think about the optimum group size for the group tasks you have in mind for students.** The most suitable group size will differ according to the nature of the task. Pairs are ideal for some tasks, while for other kinds of group work, threes, fours or fives are better. If the group is larger than about six, individuals tend to opt out or feel unable to make useful contributions to it.

4   **Give students some training in group processes.** It can be useful to use an icebreaker with the whole class, during which students work for a short while in groups, and are then briefed to analyse exactly what went well and what did not work in the group, and to identify reasons for good and bad experiences.

5   **Structure students' early attempts at group work.** It can be helpful to provide quite detailed lists of briefing instructions, and ask each group to allocate the tasks among the members. This can enable groups to work out their own directions, and then allocate them fairly in future groupwork.

6   **Help students to understand the reasons why groupwork can go wrong.** The more students know about the things that work, and the hazards of interpersonal relationships and group dynamics, the better they can cope with the aspects of human nature that inevitably play their part in any kind of group situation.

7   **Ensure that there are suitable places for students to work in groups.** Arrange that there are places where students can talk, argue and discuss things, and not just in whispers in an area that is supposed to be kept quiet. It is also useful if the groupwork venues are where students are not being observed or overheard by their tutors, or by any other groups, at least for some of the time they work together.

8   **Give students support and guidance when things go wrong.** It is not enough just to criticize a group where processes have failed; students need advice on what to do to rectify the situation, and how to handle disagreements or conflicts successfully.

9   **Be fair and firm with assessment.** Always ensure that individuals' contributions are fairly measured and assessed. Do not allow students to think that they will all earn the same mark even if they have not all made equal contributions to the work of the group. Logs of meetings, breakdowns of who agreed to do what, and evidence of the contributions that each member brought to the group, can all be prepared by students, and can all lend themselves to assessment at the end of the groupwork.

10  **Get students to evaluate the effectiveness of their groupwork.** Including such an evaluation as an assessed element in each student's work can help all of the members of a group reflect on the processes involved in their working together, and to deepen their learning about the processes involved in effective team working.

# 10

# Student group projects

Student group projects can take more care to set up and organize than individual project work, but are important as a way of getting students to develop and demonstrate important skills in working together. With large student numbers, it may not be possible to plan and assess individual project work for everyone, and group projects may help to ensure that the quality of project work remains high. Most of the considerations we offered relating to individual student projects continue to apply, and the following suggestions may help you with the particular need to get groups going successfully.

1  **Focus group project work on topics and themes where collaboration skills and team working are important.** It is unsatisfactory for students to find themselves working in groups on things that they feel they could have done as well or better by themselves.

2  **Negotiate a menu of possible outcomes for group projects with the class.** This helps students to be able to make informed choices not only about which topics they wish their group project work to address, but where possible about the constitution of the group in which they prefer to work.

3  **Try to ensure that each student group will work.** This may mean striking a balance between choosing group membership to spread out the most (and least) able students, and allowing students to work with friends.

4  **Help each student group to translate the intended outcomes of their project work into evidence specifications.** They should all be clear about the total extent and nature of the evidence that the group will aim to present for their achievements.

5  **Be clear about what will be assessed and when it will be assessed.** Sometimes the product of the overall group project will lend itself to assessment. Alternatively, it may be possible to assess individual tasks which are involved in the overall project.

6    **Try to find a range of parallel group project topics.** This can help to ensure that too many students are not competing to find or use the same resources at the same time.

7    **Help each group to divide up roles and responsibilities.** This is best done in the light of a detailed picture of the evidence which the group will be required to furnish, and students may need some help in dividing the tasks equitably and fairly among group members. Being part of this process at the outset helps you to keep track of who should be doing what, making it easier for you to spot whether the group is keeping to task or whether things are drifting.

8    **Try to ensure that everyone will participate to an equal extent.** Use group project work to give everyone involved an equivalent learning experience, though often a quite different learning experience.

9    **Allow group projects to help students to contribute on the basis of their strengths.** While it is desirable for all group members to have a go at most of the tasks that the group will tackle, it is helpful to students if they can make use of particular strengths within the group, provided that everyone can offer strengths somewhere in the overall project.

10   **Good group work does not just happen naturally.** Give groups some training in how to be effective team members. Some teambuilding exercises with the whole class, before group projects start, can alert students to some of the skills and attitudes they need to make groupwork successful.

11   **Make it clear to everyone that 'contribution' will be included in the assessment.** Students need to know in advance that there will be penalties for being a passenger. It is usual to have some form of intra-peer assessment, where students themselves decide whether or not the group members have contributed equally.

# 11

# Individual student projects

In many courses, one of the most important kinds of work undertaken by students takes the form of individual projects, often relating theory to practice beyond the college environment. Such projects are usually an important element in the overall work of each student, and are individual in nature. Setting, supporting, and assessing such work can be a major part of the work of a further education lecturer, and the following suggestions may help to make these tasks more manageable.

1   **Choose the learning-by-doing to be relevant and worthwhile.** Student projects are often the most significant and extended parts of their courses, and it is important that the considerable amount of time they may spend on them is useful to them and relevant to the overall learning outcomes of the courses or modules with which the projects are associated.

2   **Work out the specific learning outcomes for the projects.** These will often be of an individual nature for each project, as well as including general ones relating to the course area in which the project is located.

3   **Formulate projects so that they address appropriately higher level skills.** The aims of project work are often to bring together threads from different course areas or disciplines, and to allow students to demonstrate the integration of their learning.

4   **Give students as much opportunity as possible to select their own projects.** When students have a strong sense of ownership of the topics of their projects, they put much more effort into their work, and are more likely to be successful.

5   **Include scope for negotiation and adjustment of learning outcomes.** Project work is necessarily more like research than other parts of students' learning. Students need to be able to adjust the range of a project to follow

through interesting or important aspects that they discover along the way. Remember that it is still important to set standards, and the scope for negotiation may sometimes be restricted to ways that students will go about accumulating evidence to match set criteria.

6   **Make the project briefings clear, and ensure that they will provide a solid foundation for later assessment.** Criteria should be clear and well-understood by students at the start of their work on projects.

7   **Keep the scope of project work realistic.** Remember that students will usually have other kinds of work competing for their time and attention, and it is tragic when students succeed with project work, only to fail other parts of their courses that they should have devoted more time to alongside their projects.

8   **Liaise with library and information services colleagues.** When a number of projects make demands on the availability of particular learning resources or information technology facilities, it is important to arrange this in advance with these colleagues, so that they can be ready to ensure that students are able to gain access to the resources they will need.

9   **Ensure that a sensible range of factors will be assessed.** Assessment needs to relate to work that encompasses the whole of the project, and not be unduly skewed towards such skills as writing-up or oral presentation. These are likely to be assessed in any case in other parts of students' work.

10  **Collect a library of past projects.** This can be of great help to students starting out on their own projects, and can give them a realistic idea of the scope of the work likely to be involved, as well as ideas on ways to present their work well.

11  **Arrange staged deadlines for projects.** It is very useful for students to be able to receive feedback on plans for their project work, so that they can be steered away from going off on tangents, or from spending too much time on particular aspects of a project.

12  **Allow sufficient time for project work.** The outcomes of project work may well include students developing time-management and task-management skills along the way, but they need time and support to do this. Arrange contact windows so that students with problems are not left too long without help.

13   **Consider making projects portfolio-based.** Portfolios often represent the most flexible and realistic way of assessing project work, and allow appendices containing a variety of evidence to be presented along with the more important parts showing students' analysis, thinking and conclusions.

14   **Encourage students to give each other feedback on their project work.** This can be extended to elements of peer-assessment, but it is more important to get students talking to each other about their work in progress. Such feedback can help students sort out many of the problems they encounter during project work, and can improve the overall standard of their work.

15   **Think about the spaces and places which students will use to do their project work.** Some of the work might occur off-campus, but it remains important that students have access to suitable places to write up and prepare their project work for assessment, as well as facilities and support to help them analyse the data and materials they accumulate.

16   **Include a self-evaluation component in each project.** This allows students to reflect on their project work, and to think deeper about what went well and where there may have been problems. It can be particularly useful to students to get feedback about the quality of their self-evaluation.

# 12

# Involving students

The concept of 'ownership' is closely linked to effective teaching and learning. It is essentially about empowering students, and helping them to play significant roles in their own learning. The following suggestions will probably include many of the things you already do to involve students, but may give you additional ideas you can build on.

1   **Work out as many ways as possible for students to make inputs into your teaching and their learning.** For example, create an agenda for each class session, and get students to decide what they consider is the most important – and least important – item on the agenda. You may not always be able to stick exactly to the agenda that results, but it can be useful to start with the point that most students rate highly on the agenda.

2   **Show students that you value their views.** When students make suggestions that are impracticable, do not follow the urge to tell them in great detail why they would not work. Rather, ask them how they would adjust their suggestions to take into account circumstances that you know would require alternative approaches. Build on what they say, rather than destroying their confidence to make contributions.

3   **Get students to brainstorm ideas in class.** Even when starting a new topic, it can be useful to involve the class in a brainstorm to collect together all the knowledge and ideas they already have about the subject. When the session is used to develop further their ideas, their sense of ownership of the agenda helps to ensure that their concentration is maintained well.

4   **Collect feedback from students.** Do not just do this at the end of a programme of study. It is even more useful to gather interim feedback. A quick way is to ask students to make brief comments on Post-its, under the headings 'stop, start and continue'.

5   **Be seen to respond actively to any changes that appear to be wanted by your students.** This will increase their motivation. When students believe that their feedback is being ignored, they treat giving feedback as tokenistic, and it becomes much more difficult to obtain useful feedback from them in future.

6   **Involve students in setting deadlines for assessed tasks.** Students often complain that they have too many deadlines in a short period of time, and it can be useful to give them some control over at least some of these.

7   **Think of involving students in assessing some of each other's work.** Not only may this ease your assessment load (it can be much quicker to oversee peer-assessment than to do it all yourself), but also students will learn a great deal from seeing both their peers' triumphs and disasters. Equally useful is to allow students to negotiate the assessment criteria by which their individual work will be assessed.

8   **Consider letting students negotiate suitable parts of the curriculum on an individual basis.** Later in this book we give some suggestions regarding making learning agreements with students. It is useful to make the most of any opportunities to let individual students exercise their creativity and flair, and turning a suitable part of the curriculum into such opportunities pays dividends, and adds variety to your own work at the same time.

9   **Involve students in evaluating learning resource materials.** When students know that you are taking their comments and reactions seriously, they can make an excellent job of diagnosing the strengths and weaknesses of flexible learning materials and computer-based packages.

10  **Involve students in quality assurance procedures.** Students need to see that they have a valuable part to play in quality assurance, and that their views are taken into account to help design quality enhancement measures.

11  **Let students be involved in routine administrative tasks if they wish.** It can be useful to offer to groups of students responsibilities such as maintaining an attractive and uncluttered notice-board, or ringing the changes in an exhibition or gallery. It is important that students do not see such tasks as chores, and are keen to take ownership of the tasks involved.

12  **Involve students in helping each other to learn.** If a student has missed some time due to illness or injury, it can be worthwhile to ask for two or three volunteers to take the student through the main things that will have been missed. The process of coaching a fellow student is as beneficial for those doing the coaching as for the recipient.

# 13

# Using learning agreements

Learning agreements can be time-consuming to set up, particularly if you are dealing with large numbers of students. However, there are considerable advantages, and they give learners a much greater feeling of ownership of their work. Learning agreements are also an excellent vehicle for helping students to accumulate evidence directly relating to the key skill area of 'improving their own learning'. The following suggestions may help you to negotiate effective and efficient learning agreements with your students.

1   **Start with the intended learning outcomes.** These may not be particularly negotiable in themselves, but it may still be possible to allow some flexibility regarding the actual evidence that students are to produce to demonstrate their achievement of the outcomes. Remember that the outcomes must be explicit and well understood by your students in all learning agreements.

2   **Get students to think about how their work will be assessed.** It is much easier for students to put together sensible plans for individual learning agreements when they know quite a lot about the targets they are trying to reach.

3   **Let students brainstorm on the different ways that they may accumulate and present evidence of their achievement.** It is useful to do this as a class session, where students can learn from each other's ideas and approaches. They can then think about which ways they prefer to structure their own individual work to match the assessment criteria.

4   **Consider designing a proforma for each learning agreement.** This can include target dates for different stages of the work involved, as well as helping students to map the particular nature and extent of the evidence they propose to accumulate relating to the intended learning outcomes and the assessment criteria. It is useful if such proformas can be accommodated on a single side of A4 paper, so that the whole of an agreement can be viewed at once.

5    **Consider making the draft learning agreement part of the overall assessment scheme.** Even just allowing 10% of the total marks for the draft agreement enables you to give useful feedback on it, and steers students away from spending too high a proportion of their time and energy on things that could be tangential to the main purposes. Keep your own copy of each agreement, so that you are in a position to know exactly what each student is intending to achieve.

6    **Make them real agreements.** For example, when negotiating on the basis of the draft agreements, add your signature and the date, and ask students to sign alongside. Make sure that students feel genuinely involved in their agreements.

7    **Allow students to follow their individual interests within reason.** While you will still require them to produce evidence relating to central learning outcomes, there should be scope for students to make some diversions that follow up their own thoughts and ideas.

8    **Encourage students to plan staged deadlines for different parts of their work.** This helps you to be able to monitor their progress, and particularly to check up on students who may be in danger of falling too far behind in their work. It is also very useful for you to have regular opportunities to give feedback to help students avoid doing too much work on particular parts of their agreement, if other parts are being neglected.

9    **Build up a collection of learning agreements.** When you have already used learning agreements to cover a particular part of the syllabus, it can be very useful to show new students a few selected examples of previous ones, alongside the end-results that were produced by past students.

10   **Build reflection into each learning agreement.** Allocate a small but definite part of the assessment for a brief review by students on how they feel their learning agreement proceeded, from planning to implementation. Get students to review how their own learning skills have been improved by their experiences in the context of learning agreements. Such reflection can provide useful pointers on how best to approach the next set of learning agreements, both for students as they proceed to further learning agreements, and for your own planning.

# 14

# Designing effective class assignments

This is a most important part of your work, because it has strong links with your students' learning, and because it has a significant effect on your own marking workload. Assignments can serve different purposes, ranging from consolidating students' learning to assessing their knowledge and skills. The following suggestions should help ensure that your students' learning is optimized without you being completely swamped with assessment.

1   **Check carefully the links between your assignments and intended learning outcomes.** Assignments can take considerable time for your students to complete. It is important that this time is spent on tasks that are as relevant as you can make them to the topics they are learning, and to the performance criteria that you are helping them to achieve.

2   **Decide exactly what you are intending to measure.** Share the assessment criteria with your students, even before they start to undertake the assignments. When they know what they are trying to achieve, there is much more likelihood that they will structure their work efficiently, and avoid wasting time and energy on things that are not important.

3   **Go for quality rather than quantity.** It is not useful to give students the same kinds of assignment tasks repeatedly. It can be better to have a smaller overall amount of class assignment work, but to make sure that the quality of students' activity (and the relevance of the feedback that students receive) is optimal.

4   **Use class assignments to give students appropriate practice.** Design your assignments so that the learning-by-doing that students experience is useful to them in the overall context of the subjects concerned. Provide students with opportunities to practise the sorts of skills that can relate to other kinds of assessment they may face later, including exams.

5   **Use class assignments to capture students' interest.** When assignments trigger students' interest, they can improve the general level of motivation, and lead to students putting more effort into them. Avoid the sort of assignments that merely require students to write out or summarize things from source materials. Focus on ways of getting them to apply and use the information to do new or challenging thinking.

6   **Think ahead to the feedback students will receive.** It is worth working out in advance the sorts of feedback that will be most valuable to students, and planning ways to give them this feedback effectively and efficiently. Planning ahead by designing assignment return sheets, or statement banks of comments that are likely to be relevant to significant numbers of students, improves the quality and relevance of feedback to students. At the same time, such methods help you to minimize the amount of time you need to spend delivering such feedback.

7   **Consider setting staged assignments.** With essays or reports, it can be useful to allocate a small but definite proportion of the marks for an outline, or a draft, or a mental map. Giving students feedback on this 'early' thinking can help to avoid them going off on unproductive tangents as they move into the main part of their work on the assignments. Also, it does not take much of your time to give some feedback on such preliminary work if you brief students that the drafts should be on no more than one page of A4 paper.

8   **Use the benefits of peer review in class sessions.** It can be useful to get students to compare their preliminary ideas on assignment tasks, and learn from each other. This particularly helps the less able students, and does so more efficiently than if you were to try to give everyone individual feedback at this stage.

9   **Consider having a strategy involving the 'best x out of y' assignments.** This builds in a safety net for those students who may not manage to complete all of those assignments which contribute directly to their assessment. It is also useful for the most able students to have the opportunity to decide that they *only* need complete a smaller number of assignments, if their work is highly successful. This reduces the total amount of marking you need to do, and helps you direct more feedback to those students who need it most.

10  **Make good use of past assignments by other students.** It can be useful for students to see the end results of a previous batch of assignment work. Consider devoting a class session to getting students to look through an example of a good, medium, and poor past assignment, and to work out for themselves the differences between them.

# Chapter 3     Flexible Learning

Flexible learning should not be considered as separate from the various topics we have already covered under the heading 'Curriculum Delivery' in Chapter 2, as increasingly all aspects of the curriculum are being approached in flexible ways. It is no longer the case that flexible learning can be regarded as something involving a minority of students or staff, and for most students flexible learning is just as 'real' as any of the more traditional teaching–learning processes they may encounter. With the impact of information technology on the curriculum, there is also an increasing trend towards flexible modes of delivery.

In this chapter on 'flexible learning' we concentrate on various aspects of resource-based learning provision, which may be used in a variety of different ways ranging from distance learning, independent learning pathways in college-based courses, to flexible learning in learning centres and the rapidly-growing flexible learning dimensions of electronic information technology.

We begin with some primary suggestions about ways in which flexible learning can be made to succeed. This depends significantly on the appropriate selection of learning materials, either for use directly in the formats in which they are purchased, or adapted to the specific needs and requirements of your own students in the contexts of your own locality and programmes. We hope that our suggestions on adopting and adapting materials will help to save colleagues from spending too much time reinventing wheels.

Having addressed the main criteria for the quality of learning resources, we next need to look at how students are intended to learn from such materials. With the rapid growth in the range and diversity of learning resource materials, it is timely to take a more detailed look at the ways that students can best learn from them.

Next, we extend our discussion on choosing and using learning resources to take a look at the criteria that can be applied in the particular case of print-based resource materials, especially when it may be intended to issue students with their own copies of the materials to allow them to learn independently.

Learning resource centres are an increasingly important part of further education colleges' provision. We continue with some suggestions to lecturers about how they may be able to make even better use of their college's provision.

We end this chapter with just a few suggestions regarding learning from electronic sources. Such sources embrace computer-based learning materials, computer-mediated assessment programmes, and computer-generated feedback to students. They also include electronic communication between students and fellow students, and between students and tutors. Electronic sources amount to an agenda deserving a whole book to start to address it, rather than just a set of practical suggestions here. Nevertheless, we have tried to prioritize some of the main points to think about into the final section of this chapter.

# 15

# Making flexible learning work

It is increasingly usual to have flexible learning pathways or elements within normal college-based learning programmes, as well as to have flexible learning options for independent study or distance learning. The following suggestions are intended to help you make the most of the flexible learning components in your courses and programmes of study.

1    **Ensure that there is a supportive attitude towards flexible learning.** It is important that flexible learning is not seen as 'second best' to traditional teaching and learning processes or situations, but is regarded as a valid means of teaching and learning in its own right. When staff are enthusiastic about flexible learning, students' confidence levels are increased, and their expectations raised about the potential of this kind of learning for them.

2    **Provide relevant development and training both for staff and for students.** Flexible learning can be regarded as a powerful tool for helping students to learn, but such a tool can only work at its best when everyone involved knows how best to use it. Staff need to know the benefits and limitations of flexible learning, and students need to become confident enough in the processes of flexible learning to work effectively with learning resource materials.

3    **Be aware of students' expectations.** Some students (or the employers who are funding their education) may expect students to come to college to be 'taught' in traditional ways, and you should be able to explain to everyone concerned why flexible learning pathways may have replaced such traditional approaches. It is useful to highlight the benefits of developing students' autonomous learning skills, and the fact that such skills will make them better employees in due course.

4    **Work out *why* you wish to employ flexible learning approaches.** There are many good reasons for using flexible learning in specific situations, including providing equality of opportunity for students to learn in different circumstances. In particular, have good reasons for using flexible learning approaches to help students meet carefully selected learning outcomes.

5    **Target flexible learning to meet identified learning needs and outcomes.** It is best to identify the most appropriate curriculum areas for which to employ flexible learning approaches, and to do this at a course team level rather than leave it to individual lecturers.

6    **Don't drop a traditional, taught pathway too soon.** Make sure that your flexible learning pathways are tried and tested before replacing taught components. It can be particularly useful in the early stages of developing a flexible learning pathway to have this as an optional or additional way of covering the learning outcomes involved. This allows you to refine and polish the flexible learning pathway until it is good enough to replace the former way of handling that particular part of the curriculum.

7    **Express the intended learning outcomes clearly to students.** Ensure that students understand exactly what they are required to become able to do. While this is of course true of any area of the curriculum, it is particularly important where the outcomes may be delivered in print or on computer screens. It is necessary to compensate for any lack of the benefits of tone of voice, emphasis, facial expression and so on when translating the real meaning of the outcomes to students.

8    **Check carefully on what flexible learning may be replacing.** It is important that useful, shared learning experiences or attitude forming occasions are not lost. Other ways may need to be found to compensate for any lack of group interaction or tutor–student interaction that could be lost in any move towards a flexible learning element.

9    **Ensure that ongoing monitoring and support are available to students.** Some students will not find their own particular problems with flexible learning modes of study until well into their studies, and will need well-tuned support and guidance, to help them overcome such problems.

10   **Gather feedback on the processes as well as the outcomes.** It is relatively straightforward to gain feedback on the effectiveness of flexible learning pathways by analysing students' learning achievements, but it is equally important to collect feedback on how the students found their experiences of learning on such pathways.

# 16

# Adopting and adapting learning resource materials

When thinking about which learning resource materials to employ, it is useful to think carefully about whether to adopt existing materials, or whether to adapt them, or whether it may be necessary to design some new materials from scratch. The suggestions below may help you to make balanced decisions on such matters.

1   **Beware of the 'not invented here' syndrome.** It is so easy to look at a learning package (whether print-based or computer-based) and to think 'This isn't the way I would have approached this topic', or 'This contains too many things that my students don't need'. It is better to ask yourself 'Which parts of this would work well for my students?', or 'Can I give my students directions so that they can make good use of *certain* parts of the package?' Some publishers allow you to tailor their material to meet your local needs.

2   **Check the learning outcomes associated with the resource material.** Many learning resource materials present learning aims or objectives: check whether these are a good match for at least some of the learning outcomes your students need to achieve. Also check carefully whether the materials actually *deliver* the learning outcomes that they claim to.

3   **Have a go with the materials yourself.** There is no better way of finding out your first views on whether a learning package is going to be suitable for your students than to actually simulate their experience of doing the tasks yourself, and seeing whether the feedback you receive from the resource material is appropriate.

4    **Where possible, conduct a trial with students themselves.** Even if you can only do a small scale pilot, the results can be invaluable in helping you to decide whether to adopt the resource material in question, or whether it lends itself to adaptation to meet your purposes more closely.

5    **Build up your resources so that there are different ways of learning a given topic.** Students' learning approaches vary considerably, and what works for one student may not work for another. It is best when there are different options for students to choose, and when students can use one resource format to consolidate things they have learned from another kind of learning resource material.

6    **What about access and availability?** With some materials, it may be possible to give students their own copies of the materials, either wholly or in part. With other learning resources, it may only be possible for students to interact with the materials on particular workstations or equipment. Check ahead regarding the practicalities (and legalities) of getting learning resource materials into the hands of your students.

7    **Try to find out about how the materials have already worked elsewhere.** When considering the purchase of expensive resources, it is useful to have feedback on how well the materials have performed. Ask the suppliers of resources you are evaluating for contacts, so that you can approach them for data about their experience of using these materials.

8    **Look for resource materials that will save you work rather than make extra work for you.** When using resources to help your students to learn subject matter that you previously taught them in conventional ways, you need to ensure that you will not spend more time solving problems with the learning materials than you would have done if you had continued with former methods.

9    **Be willing to bypass particular parts of resource materials.** It is quite straightforward to devise briefings for students to help them to work with the most relevant parts of learning packages, and to skip entirely any areas that are not relevant to them.

10   **Think of what you may need to add.** In particular, you may need to devise additional tasks for students to do, to consolidate their learning of the most important elements of resource-based materials, and also to devise specific feedback to be available to them on such tasks.

# 17

# Helping students to learn from learning resources

The amount of resource-based learning continues to increase, not least with the growth of computer-based resource materials, and increasing use of self-study elements and flexible learning pathways. It is crucial to help students to develop their own skills and approaches so that they can make best use of such resources. The following suggestions should enable you to help your students optimize their learning from resource materials.

1   **Clarify the intended learning outcomes from each learning resource.** Many learning packages already contain learning objectives, but you may need to rearticulate and refine these in the context of the particular learning you intend your students to derive from each individual package or resource.

2   **Think ahead to what you intend to assess.** When students have a good idea about what they will be required to show for their work with a learning resource, they are better equipped to focus their work on the important parts of the resource material, and avoid being distracted by parts that may be interesting, but not sufficiently relevant.

3   **Give students the chance to develop appropriate study-skills approaches.** It can be useful to give students preliminary tasks to achieve with each of the different learning resources types they will be using, and to use these tasks to help them to develop their approaches. They may need some support, monitoring and feedback on these early explorations, and it can be useful to structure such parts of their learning outside the assessment agenda.

4   **Check out the availability of each learning resource.** Students should not have to waste time queuing for particular packages or equipment. It may be necessary to devise booking procedures so that all students have equal opportunity to work with important resources.

5   **Be aware of the danger of apparent quality.** Some learning resource materials look impressive with, for example, colourful graphics on computer screens, but it is even more important that the actual learning outcomes delivered are sound and relevant. Not all that glitters is gold!

6   **Remind students about how best they can learn from each kind of learning resource material.** It can be useful to emphasize the importance of them learning-by-doing, and making full use of the feedback which may be built into learning packages.

7   **Think about the balance between collaborative and independent work.** Especially when the availability of resource materials is limited, there can be considerable advantages in planning for collaborative learning in small groups. The assessment associated with such learning may need to point towards the independent work components, but a considerable learning payoff can be achieved collaboratively too.

8   **Help students to put resource-based learning into perspective.** Students need to know where the things they learn from resource materials fit in to the overall picture of their learning. In particular, they need to know which areas of the curriculum that they are intended to learn entirely from resource materials (as opposed to time spent on them in class), as there is a tendency for students to pick up their cues about what is important from face-to-face sessions.

9   **Monitor students' learning from resources.** It is useful to include in class assignments and course work tasks which alert you to how students' resource-based learning is proceeding. It is better to find out about any problems with the resource-based learning components at an early stage, rather than through summative assessments when it may be too late to do anything about such problems.

10  **Collect students' feedback about their experiences with learning resource materials.** Such feedback is useful when you come to review the future use of the materials, but it is also beneficial for students to reflect on how their learning has proceeded, and to compare the sorts of resource materials they feel have been most useful to them.

# 18

# Choosing print-based learning resources

The following suggestions are intended to provide an agenda of questions with which to interrogate resource materials. They can be applied both to print-based learning resource materials, and to the increasingly available 'portable electronic documents' that may be chosen to support open or flexible learning pathways for particular parts of the curriculum. It is important to make a thorough appraisal both of the nature and quality of such resource materials before buying them, and of the support that students will need when learning from such materials.

1   **Check that the published learning outcomes are relevant to your programme.** It is rare that a published package corresponds wholly to a course or section to be covered in your college. It is worth checking to what extent a package is relevant, and finding out which parts of the material may lend themselves to being used without modification or change.

2   **Ensure that the learning outcomes are clearly expressed and form a suitable basis for assessment.** You may need to rephrase the learning outcomes so that they will become a framework for you to devise assessment tasks and activities for your students, and to build in the package to other parts of your course.

3   **Check that the materials provide sufficient opportunities for learners to learn-by-doing.** To do this, look carefully at the self-assessment questions, tasks and exercises, and check that they are relevant to the learning outcomes your learners need to achieve. Check that the tasks provide suitable practice opportunities for learners, and are capable of supporting learning through making mistakes in a safe, supportive context.

4   **Ensure that learners will get good quality feedback from the materials.** Look particularly at how the materials respond to learners who have just attempted self-assessment questions and activities. They need more than just the correct answers to the questions, and need to be able to find out *why* they may have got them wrong.

5   **Will the materials enhance learners' motivation?** Are the materials attractive, stimulating and interesting, so that they will help learners to want to work through them rather than just reading them?

6   **Try to find out how well the materials have already worked elsewhere (in a similar context to yours).** Enquire about the results of piloting and trialling, and try to gather details of feedback about the materials both from learners who have used them, and tutors who have chosen them as resource materials for their students.

7   **Look for materials that can be freely copied for individual learners.** Learning tends to be more successful when learners own copies of the materials, and can write on them, particularly when answering self-assessment questions and doing tasks and exercises. It can also be desirable for learners to be able to take the materials home with them, or use them at their workplaces. Photocopiable materials can often work out far cheaper than the one-off open learning package. Such copying can make it economically practicable to use the materials with large numbers of students, and can make all the difference to individual learners who may not otherwise be able to do the programme of study.

8   **Work out whether the materials will be self-sufficient.** Some learning resource packages can be used without any supporting materials, while others depend on the availability of particular reference sources or textbooks. If additional materials are needed to accompany the packages, check both the cost and availability of these materials.

9   **Will learners need ongoing tutor support?** Some materials contain sufficient feedback to learners so that they can work through them without additional support, but most materials really need learners to have formative feedback on tutor-marked assignments at various stages of their work. Be realistic about the tutor support that may be required, and allow time and costing for this when planning how to make use of learning packages.

10  **Do the materials contain overall assessment tasks that can be used directly?** Or might it be preferable to compose college specific assessment tasks and processes to measure learners' work when they have completed their work through the packages?

# 19

# Making the most of learning centres

With the rapid development both of the quantity and quality of learning resource materials, students do an increasing proportion of their learning in learning resource centres. There has emerged a twin model of provision of such centres, with central facilities in colleges being supplemented by satellite or specialist centres in particular departments. The following suggestions should help you to optimize the learning payoff associated with such provision.

1   **Get to know what your own college already has.** Find out where your learning centres are, and what they cover, and how the materials are designed to work. Check opening hours, and any particular timetabling features, such as early closing on certain days or times of the year, or whether the centres are block-booked for particular groups of students at certain times.

2   **Avoid the view that learning centres are just well-equipped libraries.** Familiarize yourself, if necessary, as to how flexible learning is intended to work. Look broadly at how the centres can best help your own students to learn. Make sure your students get a sound induction of how to make the most of the resources available to them.

3   **Get yourself timetabled into the centre.** Plan to be there yourself, and to work with your students as they familiarize themselves with the packages and materials they will use. Don't just abandon them to work on their own during such timetabled sessions. Once they develop the skills to work without much direct support from you, you can always take other work of your own into the centre at such times.

4   **Look carefully at the 'how to use this' instructions.** Improving and developing such instructions will help your students work better on their own, and will save you time and energy explaining the same things repeatedly to individual students. It is also worth encouraging students to help each other on how to use new kinds of resources. Someone who has just learned how to use a resource successfully is often the best person to explain it to someone just starting to use it.

5   **Work collaboratively with the staff in the centre.** They can be of great help in alerting you to the resources you can exploit. Tell them what you need, and explain the context in which your students are learning the topics covered by the resource materials. Get the staff involved in your proposed activities in the centre, and liaise specifically with them regarding the assessment briefings that you will issue to students relating to the work they do there.

6   **Use the staff to help you develop or extend your own learning materials.** They can give invaluable help in editing materials you already have, or converting them towards new resource-based learning packages. They can also help you to begin developing new materials, and advise or get involved in the production of print-based or electronic materials.

7   **Monitor carefully the links between the learning that students undertake in resource centres and their development of key skills.** Students may be able to derive important evidence for their development of key skills in the context of their work in resource centres. It may be useful to liaise on this with any specialist tutors or learning skills development colleagues who are also involved in the work of the centre, and these colleagues may be able to work in partnership with you on suitable areas of the centre's provision.

8   **Make the most of the technology available.** Learning resource centres may be the ideal vehicle for helping your students develop information technology skills and accumulate evidence of these skills. Consider the potential of supporting students by electronic means, such as e-mail. Help your students become familiar and fluent with multimedia provision. Think of the possibilities of extending student support and media-based learning to distant students in networked centres elsewhere.

9   **Consider what you can put *in* to the centre.** The centre may be an ideal repository for some of your own learning materials, and even for 'locked away' textbooks and resources which could be made available to more students.

10   **Review the things you still cover in classrooms and workshops.** Remain on the lookout for areas of learning which might be better located or better supported in a learning resource centre. It is valuable to extend the usage of such centres, as this helps to justify future expenditure on resources, particularly those that will be of value to a wide range of students studying different disciplines.

# 20

# Learning from electronic sources

Electronic sources are becoming much more widely used, and students usually take every opportunity to play with new information technology spin-offs. Sadly, the new technologies do not always seem to be used to best effect when the intention is focused learning or communication. When the aim is for such media to be part of students' study resources, we have to take care that their *learning* is structured as much as possible. Whether using the Internet, or a local Intranet of networked computer terminals, we need to ensure that students' actions are productive and focused. The suggestions below are intended to be just a starting point.

1 **Don't just make traditional material available electronically.** It is of very limited value putting straight lecture notes onto an Intranet or even on the Internet. Such materials rarely lend themselves to being seen on monitor screens, where only a small part of the whole might be visible at a time. If the only way for students to handle the materials is to print them off and then learn from them in traditional ways, it is worth thinking twice before making the material available electronically.

2 **Be wary about overwhelming your students with information.** The amount of material available to students through their computer screens grows exponentially. The quantity of information that students can be exposed to in a 'sitting' is vastly more than that which may have been covered by a lecturer in a lecture.

3 **Work out the intended learning outcomes.** When students are interrogating electronic materials, it is more important than ever that they know what they are looking for. They need to be able to make sensible decisions regarding what to scan, what to keep, and what to ignore. Carefully formulated learning outcomes can alert students to the agenda for their usage of electronic sources.

4   **Help students to develop 'search and select' skills.** Whether working from an electronic database or from the Internet, it is vital that students know how to find the *relevant* material for their purposes. Searching for relevant and useful information within a reasonable time period is an advanced skill. You must be prepared to give your students plenty of support and guidance on this.

5   **Help students to develop a critical perspective.** Electronic sources are no different from traditional print-based ones in that the authors' biases, inaccuracies or lack of currency can affect the reliability with which the resource may be used. The authenticity and quality of textbooks and journal articles may be guaranteed by the editorial and review processes prior to publication. Because of the immediacy and democracy of the Internet, there may not be such guarantees.

6   **Build in plenty of activity.** Students will soon become bored if all they are doing is pointing and clicking. Give them small tasks, tests and quizzes, and opportunities to reflect upon what they have learned. Look for ways in which the medium provides students with genuinely interactive learning experiences.

7   **Look ahead to what you are going to assess.** Start by working out what it is *possible* to assess. It is of limited value simply getting students to use electronic sources, unless you have decided how you can measure the quality of their usage. Work out the kinds of *evidence* from which the quality and effectiveness of students' usage of electronic sources can be quantified.

8   **Use each medium to do the things that it does well.** Use electronic media to avoid replicating effort, to save multiple postal mailings, to deliver volumes of material that would be expensive to copy onto paper, and to communicate when speed is crucial.

9   **When developing your own materials, write to match the medium.** The best web-based materials are accessible and punchy, use short sentences, lots of bullet points, and user-friendly language.

10  **Think how you will make your own screen-based materials visually interesting.** Explore your capacity to use graphics, video clips, colour and images of all kinds to help students to feel excited about their learning materials. Check that the workstations your students will be using will support your materials.

11   **Be aware of copyright problems.** This is still a minefield, so be cautious about doing anything you would hesitate to do on paper for copyright reasons. This includes cutting and pasting extracts from other electronic sources.

12   **Be aware that effective computer-based learning materials take time to develop.** Estimates of 100 developer-hours per hour of student learning are not unusual. Allow for this in your development plans. However, hardware, software, and 'wet ware' (human brain activity) is developing all the time, and will certainly continue to bring the development time down.

13   **Look at what is already available.** Lots of 'lone heroes' have produced computer-based learning materials, often in isolation, and it is tragic not to make use of other people's hard-won achievements. Lots of useful materials have been developed in isolation, and it important to seek every opportunity to adapt or adopt them where they are relevant.

14   **Remember that computer-based learning materials need updating.** Just as with any other curriculum delivery mechanism, computer-based learning materials need to be reviewed regularly and revised as situations and contexts change. Fortunately, this is now fairly easy to do with information technology based systems, so be willing to update materials as often as you feel is necessary.

15   **Get your students to help you make the materials better.** Many of our younger students learned information technology skills soon after they learned to walk, so they are likely to be very familiar with what works and what does not work on-screen. Ask such students to evaluate your computer-based learning packages, and note carefully both their criticisms and their praise.

16   **Help students to use electronic communication effectively.** This means not just making sure that they know how to log on and send or receive messages. Students may need guidance about how to ensure that electronic communications get their messages across effectively. Help them to keep messages concise and clear, and set an example with your own electronic messages. Be careful, however, not to patronize or undervalue those students who are already skilled at electronic communication.

17   **Look for ways of using electronic communication to save you time and energy.** For example, consider using computer conferences to give general feedback to a large class on your marking of their reports or essays. Personal e-mail to individual students can then give them additional direct feedback about the strengths and weaknesses of their work.

18  **Consider using computer conferencing methods as a means of course delivery.** With large classes or dispersed groups of distance learners this can be very effective, and can make up for the more limited opportunities of face-to-face sessions. The evidence suggests that more reserved students find it less daunting to ask questions by e-mail and find it easier to participate in 'virtual' group activities. Interaction is improved as students seem better able to make sense of discussions, by rereading items as often as they need to before making their own contributions or responses.

19  **Ensure that students have adequate access to electronic sources.** If progress or assessment depends on having access, make sure that such access is generous. There is already evidence that student appeals against assessment decisions are being based on claims that access to particular resources was not sufficiently possible.

20  **Don't expect to do away with face-to-face time altogether.** Human interaction is often one of the key elements that students report as helping them to learn. The virtual tutor should not totally replace the human one in most overall learning contexts.

# Chapter 4   Assessment Strategies

Assessment is the most important thing we ever do for our students as it can be the aspect of our work that affects students' whole lives and careers. Assessment is also a very significant part of our workload as further or continuing education lecturers, and it is important that we make this part of our work not only effective but efficient. Furthermore, assessment is a powerful driving force for student learning, and we need to make best use of this to ensure that the assessment processes and instruments we devise contribute fully towards optimizing the quality and depth of our students' learning experience.

We begin this chapter with some principles on which we advocate effective assessment should be based. We continue by revisiting the very purposes of assessment. In 'Why should we assess?', we point towards the need to have better thought out strategies than would be simply the consequence of answers along the lines of 'because it's always been done this way'.

Having established good reasons for assessing, the next priority becomes *what* to assess. We offer some suggestions to help you to check that your assessment processes and the instruments used for measuring them match the learning outcomes that you intend your students to achieve.

Having addressed the questions 'why?' and 'what?', the next question is *'how?'* We offer some thoughts on factors to bear in mind when choosing which of the many possibilities to use for methods of assessment on each occasion.

This paves the way to our suggestions about adopting a strategic approach to assessment in the broad context of an institution, and next to the individual situation of a particular course or programme area.

We continue with suggestions about 'Making assessment manageable'. However desirable an innovative form of assessment may be, or conducive to deep learning by students it may prove, it is unlikely to get beyond the planning stage unless it is manageable both for staff and students.

Assessment and record-keeping go hand in hand, and our next set of suggestions offers some general advice about 'Keeping track of assessment'.

We end this chapter with a set of suggestions about the most important aspect of assessment, when thinking about learning improvement: feedback to students. This is also the aspect of assessment that can be most time intensive for lecturers, and as it is so important to students, it is vital that the time spent by lecturers on giving feedback to students on their assessed work is worthwhile, significant, and well-focused.

# 21

# Principles of assessment

We believe that assessment should be driven by values that ensure that it is of appropriate quality and will fit the purposes for which it is designed. The following principles aim to help lecturers to ensure that all assessment practices and procedures, whether designed in college or dictated by external bodies or agencies, are sound and workable.

1   **Assessment should be valid.** It should assess what it is that you really want to measure. For example, when attempting to assess problem solving skills, the assessment should not be dependent on the quality and style of the production of written reports on problem solving, but on the quality of the solutions devised.

2   **Assessment should be reliable.** If we can get right the task briefings, assessment criteria and marking schemes, there should be good inter-tutor reliability when more than one tutor marks the work, as well as good intra-tutor reliability (tutors themselves should come up with closely matching results when marking the same work on different occasions).

3   **Assessment should promote equality of opportunity.** Students should have equality of opportunities to succeed given that their experiences are rarely identical. This is particularly important when assessing work based in individual learning contracts. It is also important that all assessment instruments and processes should *be seen to be fair* by all students.

4   **Assessment should offer a 'level playing field'.** Assessment methods should not ultimately favour any particular individual or group, simply because of the method chosen. Obviously, students may prefer and do better at different kinds of assessment (some love exams and do well in them, while others are better at giving presentations) so a balance of different means of assessment within a course will ensure that no particular group is favoured above any other group.

5    **Assessment should be formative.** Assessment is a time-consuming process for all concerned, so it seems like a wasted opportunity if it is not used as a means of letting students know how they are doing and how they can improve. Assessment that is primarily summative in its function (such as when only a number or grade is given) gives students very little information, other than frequently confirming their own prejudices about themselves.

6    **Assessment should be timely.** Assessment that occurs only at the end of a learning programme is not much use in providing feedback, and also leads to the 'sudden death' syndrome, where students have no chance to practise before they pass or fail. Even where there is only end-point formal assessment, earlier opportunities should be provided for rehearsal and feedback.

7    **Assessment should be incremental.** Ideally, feedback to students should be continuous and available to students at a time when it can help them improve. There is sense, therefore, in enabling small units of assessment to build up into a final mark or grade. This avoids surprises, and can be much less stressful than systems when the whole programme rests on performance during a single time limited occasion.

8    **Assessment should be redeemable.** Where possible, students should have opportunities for the redemption of failure when things go wrong. This is not only just, but avoids high attrition rates which can affect funding.

9    **Assessment should be demanding, but attainable.** Assessment systems should not be seen by students to be too simple, and the assurance of quality is impossible when students are not stretched by assessment methods. That is not to say that systems should only permit a fixed proportion of students to achieve each grade: a good assessment system should permit all students considered capable of undertaking a course of study to have a chance of succeeding in the assessment, provided they learn effectively and work hard.

10   **Assessment should be efficient.** Brilliant systems of assessment can be designed, but which are completely unmanageable because of ineffective use of staff time and resources. The burden on staff should not be excessive, nor should be the demands on students undertaking the assessment tasks.

# 22

# Why should we assess?

If we think clearly about our reasons for assessment, it helps to clarify which particular methods are best suited for our purposes, as well as helping to identify who is best placed to carry out the assessment, and when and where to do it. Assessment should not be seen as an end in its own right, but should be delivering useful learning payoff to students in all three stages involved: preparation for assessment, being assessed, and receiving feedback on their work. Some of the most common reasons for assessing students are referred to below. It is worth noting that many of the reasons we suggest can also be used to explain the purposes of assessment to students themselves, while one or two are necessarily connected more directly to the functions of the college.

1  **To guide improvement.** This is probably the single most important reason for using assessment. The feedback students receive helps them to improve. Assessment that is primarily formative need not necessarily count towards any final award and can, therefore, be ungraded in some instances. The more detailed the feedback we provide, the greater is the likelihood that students will have opportunities for further development.

2  **To enable student progression.** Students often cannot undertake a course of study unless they have a sound foundation of prior knowledge or skills. Assessment methods to enable student progression need to give a clear idea of students' current levels of achievement, so they – and we – can know if they are ready to progress. Assessment should help to ensure that students are placed on the most appropriate courses, from which they will be able to benefit.

3  **To facilitate students' choice of options.** If students have to select options within a programme, an understanding of how well (or otherwise) they are doing in their studies will enable them to have a firmer understanding of their current abilities in different subject areas. This can provide them with guidance on which options to select next.

4    **To classify or grade students.** There are frequently pressures on us to classify the level of achievements of students individually and comparatively within a cohort. The outside world seems to be preoccupied with measures of students' performance relative to each other, even when such data do not tell the whole story. Assessment methods to achieve this will normally be summative and involve working out numerical marks or letter grades for students' work of one kind or another.

5    **To diagnose faults and enable students to rectify mistakes.** Nothing is more demotivating than struggling on, getting bad marks and not knowing what is going wrong. Effective assessment lets students know where their problems lie, and provides them with an essential understanding of the tools available to put things right.

6    **To give us feedback on how our teaching is going.** If there are generally significant gaps in student knowledge, this often indicates faults in the teaching in the areas concerned. Excellent achievement by a high proportion of students is often due to high quality facilitation of student learning.

7    **To motivate students.** As students find themselves under increasing pressure, they tend to become more strategic in their approaches to learning, only putting their energies into work that counts. Assessment methods can be designed to maximize student motivation, and prompt their efforts towards important achievements.

8    **To provide statistics for the course, or for the institution.** Colleges need to provide funding agencies with data about student performance, and assessment systems need to take account of the need for appropriate statistical information.

9    **To consolidate learning.** Students often do not feel they have really learned something until they have had the opportunity to demonstrate what they can do within an assignment. Assessment can provide opportunities for students to apply abstract concepts to practical contexts in ways that makes the learning meaningful to them.

10    **To add variety to students' learning experience, and add direction to our teaching.** Utilizing a range of different assessment methods spurs students to develop different skills and processes. This can provide more effective and enjoyable teaching and learning.

# 23

# Working out what you really want to assess

Very often, we find that we are assessing not what we really want to assess, but what happens to be easy to assess. 'If you can assess it, it probably isn't it' is one way of summarising the dilemma. It is important, therefore, to be very clear about what we are actually committed to assess. To set you thinking, ask yourself the following questions about each assessment task you use; they are designed to help you make the right assessment decisions for your context. The way we have written these questions may suggest certain polarities to you, but your answers may well lie halfway along the spectrum in many cases.

1   **Is it product or process that is to be assessed?** Are we concentrating in this particular assessment task on the actual outcome (maybe a report, essay, or artefact), or are we looking at how the students achieved the outcome?

2   **Is it specific subject knowledge that we test, or is it how well students can use such information?** Does the method of assessment prioritize the need for information recall and regurgitation, or is the knowledge involved needed as a background for synthesis, analysis and evaluation by students?

3   **Is it individual effort or team effort that is to be assessed?** Teamwork is valued by employers, tutors and the students themselves, and sometimes it is most appropriate to assess students in groups. On other occasions, the performance of individuals needs to be very clearly differentiated.

4   **Is it teaching or learning that is being assessed?** Are the assessment tasks teacher-centred or student-centred? Are the tasks designed to allow students to demonstrate to what extent their learning has succeeded?

5    **Is assessment primarily formative or summative?** Are marks or grades needed by students at this point, or is this assessment task primarily there to allow students to receive feedback? There is little point writing detailed comments on the written work of students about to leave the college if they will never be able to read them!

6    **Is the assessment convergent or divergent?** Are all students aiming to achieve identical results ('right answers'), or are the assessment tasks designed to enable students to demonstrate individuality and diversity? Both approaches may well be appropriate within a given course at different stages.

7    **Is the methodology continuous or end-point?** If it is continuous, there may be opportunities for redemption of failure without the risk of any particular element of assessment being too high. If assessment methodology is end-point, then students will need to be made aware of this and prepared for it.

8    **Does the assessment encourage deep, surface, or strategic learning?** Encouraging deep learning has implications for curriculum design. When students are over-assessed, most will learn at a surface or strategic level only.

9    **Is the assessment holistic or serialist?** Does the assignment give students an opportunity to integrate material from a variety of sources, or is it a discrete element, relating to a specific aspect of learning? Which approach is the most appropriate for the context in which you are working?

10    **Is the assessment time/context specific, or is it ipsative? (ie a measure of improvement).** Does it measure achievement at a fixed point in time, or the extent of individuals' development from their earlier starting points?

11    **Is the assessment norm-referenced or criterion-referenced?** Does it measure a student's achievement in relation to that of other students, or does it enable students' achievements to be measured against a set of criteria? In the first instance, there is a tendency to have fixed pass/fail rates, whereas with criterion referencing, everyone who achieves the criteria will have passed.

# 24

# Choosing the most appropriate methods of assessment

The range of assessment methods to choose from is much wider than is often realized. Yet a great deal of assessment in colleges is limited to essays, reports, and traditional time-constrained exams. Many college programmes do not permit flexibility in choice of assessment method as these are externally decided, but, where there are such opportunities, we would encourage you to use them to the full. These questions aim to stimulate your thinking and help you choose the best method of assessment appropriate to your context, your students, the level, the subject and the college.

1  **Which, if any, of the following written elements should you choose from?** Consider the best uses of essays, reports, reviews, summaries, dissertations, annotated bibliographies, case studies, journal articles, presentations, and exams of all kinds, including takeaway papers and open-book exams.

2  **Should the method be time-constrained?** Exams, phase tests and classroom activities might well be the most appropriate for the occasion. Time constrained tests put students under pressure and often place heavy reliance on basic information recall, but are usually fairly good at preventing cheating, are easy to administer and familiar to many students and staff.

3  **Is it important that the method you choose includes cooperative activity?** If it is important, you might choose to assess students in groups, perhaps on group projects, poster displays or presentations. You might consider including an element of peer assessment to enable you to get a fair assessment of group process. When assessing students in groups, decide how you will discriminate between individuals' performances within the group if it is to be seen to be fair.

4    **Is a visual component required?** When it is required, you might choose portfolios, poster displays, 'critique' sessions or exhibitions. Obviously there are resource implications that need to be taken into account in terms of materials and display space.

5    **Is it important that students use information technology?** When it is important, computer-based assessments might be best carried out on PCs or networked systems. You can consider getting students to answer multiple-choice questions, with or without feedback loops, or ask them to write their own programmes, prepare databases, write information stacks for hypertext, or material for use in CD-ROM systems or on the Internet. Resource implications are important here too, and you will need to consider how best to ensure the security of your methodology against cheating and impersonation.

6    **Do you wish to try to assess innovation or creativity?** Some assessment methods that allow students to demonstrate these include performances, exhibitions, poster displays, presentations, projects, student-led assessed seminars, simulations and games. Developing appropriate assessment criteria for something like 'flair' that are explicit yet non-directive is a difficult task, so you should involve students fully in the process so they can understand the mechanisms by which decisions are made.

7    **Are you keen to encourage students to develop oral skills?** If so, you might choose to assess vivas, presentations, recorded elements of audio and video tapes made by students, assessed discussions or seminars, interviews or simulations. It is especially important to make sensible decisions concerning timing of assessments where individual oral performance is involved, to avoid lecturer and student exhaustion.

8    **Do you want to assess the ways in which students interact together?** You might assess negotiations, debates, role plays, interviews, selection panels, and case studies. Clear, available and preferably negotiated criteria are important to ensure students have confidence in the way in which they are being assessed.

9    **Is the assessment of learning that occurs away from the institution important?** You may wish to assess learning done in the work place, in professional contexts or on field courses. You may choose to assess logs, reflective journals, critical incident accounts, field study diaries, annotated maps, case studies or portfolios.

10   **Is your aim to establish what students are able to do already?** Then you could try diagnostic tests (paper-based or technology-based), profiles, records of achievement, portfolios, interviews, and vivas.

# 25

# Adopting a strategic approach to assessment

Assessment is one of the most valuable and important parts of college lecturers' tasks and yet it is often the most burdensome. Further education lecturers may be involved in designing the strategies with which assessment is handled, when colleges adopt a policy of involving lecturers in such overall strategy matters. Managing the way in which we assess can make a difference to the efficiency of the way we approach it and can lead to higher levels of consistency of marking. These tips are designed to help course teams to prioritize what they feel are the most important aspects of assessment and to enable effective and collaborative working.

1   **Why develop a college assessment strategy?** Often assessment practices in colleges have evolved rather than being devised. A strategy can help ensure a coherent approach across the college, and make it easier to provide equivalence of experience for students. A strategy can also cater for ways of sharing best practice, so that mutual professional development can occur. An assessment strategy can be designed to cover issues such as ensuring that an appropriately diverse range of assessment methods are used, and to balance the relationship between formative feedback and summative assessment.

2   **Who should write the strategy?** Ownership of a college-wide assessment strategy is more likely to occur if people from throughout the college are involved in devising it. It is worth thinking carefully about representation. A mixture of policy makers and grass roots lecturers is usually the best combination. It also makes sense to look at the policies of other colleges, and to build on their better elements.

3   **Anticipate the occurrences of cheating, and students 'playing the system'.** Unfortunately students will sometimes be tempted to circumvent your assessment systems. It is, therefore, important for everyone to be clear about the sanctions that are available within your institution. Equally, your students should be aware of the consequences of cheating or playing the system. It can be worth building in such factors to student contracts. As institutions bring in students from a wider economic, social and cultural range, problems relating to interpretation of assessment systems are likely to increase. A strategic approach to assessment needs not only to address the robustness of the assessment processes, but also to address what should be done when things go wrong.

4   **Once there is a draft strategy, advocate wide consultation about it.** Even though such consultation may delay implementation, it is worth the time and energy needed for effective consultation. This allows the strategy to be placed on the agenda of department meetings to enable discussion by all involved in its implementation. You will also need to consult external bodies such as partners in higher education, exam boards and accreditation agencies.

5   **Rank and file staff support is the critical element.** Staff may only pay lip service to any policy on assessment unless they have a healthy feeling of ownership of the processes and methods involved in the strategy. It is worth incorporating suggestions from as many members of staff as possible, while ensuring that the strategy remains coherent and practicable.

6   **Where possible, ensure that student opinion has been canvassed.** Students rightly feel very strongly about assessment. Listen to their views carefully and be seen to act on them. A policy backed by students is far easier to implement.

7   **Work out how best to communicate the strategy to staff and students.** Use all available means to communicate the main points, including staff and student newsletters, college documentation of all kinds. Also consider using electronic means of communication such as e-mail and electronic bulletin boards where these are available.

8   **Plan to ensure that the strategy will be implemented fully.** This is the hardest part. The best approach is to set target dates to build up a staged implementation, with frequent opportunities to review and discuss learning points found during the implementation, and to fine-tune the strategy to take account of experiences gained.

9  **Consider the implications for on-going staff development.** An assessment workshop, internally or externally facilitated, can be valuable for sharing ideas, strategies and anxieties. Think carefully about who should attend such workshops, and what the intended outcomes should be.

10  **Be aware of the resource implications of your assessment strategy.** Think about the costs of staff time release, developmental activities and production of documentation. Cost these realistically and make a case for your strategy. When college management is really committed to a strategy, the resources needed are more likely to be forthcoming.

11  **Expect the policy to be a dynamic document.** It will need to develop as circumstances change. Be prepared to evaluate and revise the policy as appropriate. Build in an evaluation strategy from the beginning, and do not be afraid to make modifications on the basis of experience to keep the policy alive.

12  **Keep the main implementation documentation short and sharp.** Build in the extra detail addressing all the 'what if..?' questions in appendices and annexes, so you do not lose the interest of the busy people who will be reading the document.

# 26

# Course or programme area assessment strategies

Colleagues working together in course or programme teams are well placed to adopt a strategic approach to assessment. The most effective way of introducing major improvements in assessment is when they are planned at this level. We present below some questions which may make useful starting points for team discussions about assessment.

1   **How can you ensure that assessment is addressed as an integral part of quality review?** Does your team review the effectiveness of assessment on an annual basis? Is internal review considered as important as external moderation? How much responsibility is taken at a local level for good assessment practice?

2   **Are relevant assessment criteria identified and used by all colleagues assessing any given assignment?** Discussing criteria in a team usually leads to clarification and simplification of the criteria, making it easier for staff to understand and use them as well as to explain them to students in meaningful ways.

3   **Are the reasons for the choice of assessment methods transparent to everyone?** It is important that they are not only understood by staff and students, but also by employers, accrediting agencies, higher education partners and other people who may need to know exactly what is being measured and how it is being approached.

4   **Are assessment workloads realistic?** Are the allocated assessment workloads equitably and sensibly apportioned? Can students and staff cope with them? It can be very useful to plot likely workloads for staff and students when planning assignments, so that you can predict times of difficulty and warn both groups to plan their time accordingly.

5   **Are the assessment tasks practicable?** Can they be completed with the available resources? For example, do students have sufficient access to computers, learning materials, and other resources they may need?

6   **Have other stakeholders been consulted and heeded?** It is well worth building in the advice which can be obtained from study-skills support staff, library staff, learning resources centre personnel, and so on.

7   **Are the assessments suitable for all students?** Check that tasks and assignment content are equally appropriate for males and females in their content and format. Do not always use results from male-dominated sports in statistics examples. Try to ensure that the assessments do not discriminate between students with different racial, cultural or language contexts. For example, avoid always using UK companies as case studies in business studies assignments, which are likely to privilege those with local background knowledge.

8   **Is the range of assessment methods used by your team sufficiently broad?** Try to ensure that all students have a mixed range of assessment methods. This will help to accommodate students' differences in learning styles. A diverse range of assessment methods allows students who struggle with one particular kind of assessment to show their strengths through other types. Students should not be repeatedly penalized when they happen to have difficulties with a specific assessment format, such as time-constrained written exams.

9   **Do you monitor the time spent on assessment tasks of all kinds?** Do you try to work out how much time is devoted to providing feedback, compared to the time involved in setting and marking work, attending assessment boards, and keeping assessment records? Are you happy with the balance of activities? Are concerns fed back to the course teams, or the college management, when appropriate?

10  **Are you confident that you are assessing what you claim you do in course documentation?** Are you confident that where the curriculum is expressed in terms of learning outcomes, you test them appropriately? If you ask these questions, you can help your team to tease out some aspects of learning which may be hard to assess, but where it is really important to try to do so.

11  **Has due consideration been given regarding when to assess?** Try to avoid students becoming overburdened with assessed tasks at particular parts of the term, semester or year. It is worth asking whether assessment should be timed for when students are ready for it, or as a driving force to help them to achieve the learning outcomes at a particular time.

12  **Have appropriate roles been devised for internal and/or external verifiers?** Is the feedback from such people used appropriately to help with self-assessment of provision, and fed into college-wide quality assurance and quality enhancement provision?

13  **How do you monitor the effectiveness and reliability of your assessment?** Do you keep good statistical records which enable you to compare student performance against their base line ability at college entry? Does your strategy allow you to explore how much improvement or development there has been, that is to say, how far individual students have progressed and can demonstrate added value?

# 27

# Making assessment manageable

Many more college teachers are finding that the burden of assessment is becoming difficult to manage. Formative assessment is one of the best ways of promoting student learning, but as student numbers rise and class sizes grow larger, we have to look at ways of coping with the greater workloads of assessment, without short changing students. We offer a number of strategies.

1   **Where possible, reduce the number of assignments.** Especially following changes in course design, we often find ourselves assessing larger numbers of assignments. We can ask ourselves if all of these are strictly necessary, and whether it is possible to combine some of them and completely delete others.

2   **Go for quality instead of quantity.** Remind yourself of all the purposes you wish your assessments to serve, particularly those relating to giving students useful feedback and helping them to structure their future learning in a more focused way. A smaller number of assignments can serve these purposes much better than when assessment and feedback become rushed because of the sheer volume of work involved.

3   **Consider developing cross-theme assignments.** These can lessen the burden of assessment both for students and for staff, and can be a way of incorporating the assessment of key skills into the curriculum in an integrated and natural way.

4.  **Consider reducing or removing the word-length requirement on assignments.** The 2,000 to 3,000 word assignment is often a fairly automatic expectation, yet half the length could be just as acceptable if the content were adapted accordingly. This does not mean that students should be advised to 'stop when you have written x number of words' but they could be asked to provide bullet points or summaries instead of full assignments.

5    **Consider the benefits of tutoring during the growth of project-type assignments.** Monitoring the development of such assignments over a period of time, and helping students tune their work to the required standard, dramatically reduces the time needed to assess the finished products. The burden of assessing such assignments is reduced especially if good records are maintained after each tutorial session or intervention.

6    **Use assignment return sheets.** These can be proformas which contain the assessment criteria for an assignment, with spaces for ticks/crosses, grades, marks and brief comments. They enable rapid feedback on routine assessment matters, providing more time for individual comment to students when necessary on deeper aspects of their work. Using multipart formats for such data saves copying time and helps keep track of students' progress.

7    **Consider using statement banks.** These are a means whereby frequently-repeated comments can be listed on a sheet of paper to be stapled to student work, or put onto overhead transparencies for discussion in a subsequent lecture. For more detail on these see Brown, Rust and Gibbs (1994).

8    **Think about different kinds of assignment.** Perhaps some essays or long reports could be replaced by shorter reviews, articles, memorandum-reports or summaries. Projects could perhaps be assessed by poster displays instead of long written assignments, and exam papers could include some sections of multiple-choice questions, particularly where these could be marked by optical mark scanners or optical character recognition systems. When computer-assisted assessment processes are not available for marking multiple-choice papers, an effective simple alternative is to use overhead transparencies with the correct answers 'ringed' to overlay onto scripts as an aid to rapid manual marking.

9    **Involve students in peer-assessment.** Start small, and explain what you are doing and why. Peer-assessment can provide students with very positive learning experiences. At the start, it can be less threatening for students to assess anonymous work from a previous cohort.

10   **Encourage student self-assessment.** This is a most valuable skill in its own right for students to acquire. It is useful to give students some feedback on how well they have done self-assessment. It is quicker to monitor student self-assessment than to do all the assessment yourself.

11 **Mark some exercises in class time using self- or peer-grading.** Where you can provide correct or model answers, students can gain great benefit from comparing their work with them and learning to make accurate self-judgements of their work Assessing learning in such ways in class gives time and opportunity for valuable debates about criteria and standards.

12 **Don't measure the same thing time and time again.** Collaborate with colleagues on other courses, look for overlaps between assignments, and agree where these can be integrated.

# 28

# Keeping track of assessment

Because assessment is one of the most important tasks we do, it is important that we keep good records of this aspect of our work. This takes time, but can save time and problems in the long run. The following suggestions may help you organize your record-keeping.

1   **Be meticulous.** However tired you are at the end of a marking session, record all the marks immediately (or, indeed, continuously as you go along). Then put the marks in a different place to the scripts. Then should any disasters befall you (car containing scripts stolen, house burned down and so on) there is the chance that you will still have the marks even if you do not have the scripts any longer (or vice versa).

2   **Be systematic.** Use class lists, when available, as the basis of your records. Otherwise make your own class lists as you go along. File all records of assessment in places where you can find them again. It is possible to spend as much time looking for missing marksheets as it took to do the original assessment.

3   **Use technology to produce assessment records.** Keep marks as spreadsheets or databases on a computer, and save by date as a new file every time you add to it, so you are always confident that you are working with the most recent version. Remember to keep paper copies of each list as an insurance against disaster.

4   **Use technology to save you from number-crunching.** The use of computer spreadsheet programs can allow the machine to do all of the sub-totalling, averaging and data handling for you. If you are afraid to set up a system for yourself, a computer-loving colleague may be delighted to start you off. It is well worth checking results manually from time to time, to ensure that the computer is crunching your numbers according to your intentions.

5   **Make sure you use the college support system.** Many colleges require course administration records to be stored in secure, centralized places. Work with your course administration colleagues to keep the necessary records of students' progress. Colleges are increasingly using networked computerized student tracking systems such as 'ROCKET'.

6   **Keep your own copies of all assessment data.** This applies whether the data are on paper or on disk. Simply photocopying a handwritten list of marks is a valuable precaution. Remind yourself how serious it would be if some of your records of assessment were irretrievably lost. Never trust anyone, even your dearest colleague, with the only copy of your marks.

7   **Keep files, not piles.** Consider keeping a progress file for each student (or for each group), as well as a file showing all the data for each assignment by hand-in date. Make use of any pre-printed marking grids, multipart assessment sheets, and so on, where such materials are available to you. If such devices are not available, consider designing your own.

8   **Post on-going assessment grids on your office door or on a student notice board.** This not only helps you keep up your records, but spurs on students who are late submitting work when they see gaps alongside their names.

9   **Deal effectively with late assignments.** It is particularly important to have a system for dealing with students who habitually miss hand-in dates, and ensuring that such students are treated similarly across all of the courses or modules they may be taking.

10  **Keep to turn-round schedules.** It is important that students know when their work will be marked and returned to them, and that these schedules are seen to be adhered to by all of the staff who assess their work.

11  **Involve students.** Give students a full print-out of the mark sheet after each piece of work has been returned to a class, and let them check their own scripts against the master copy. When working with large groups, it is only too easy to transpose marks accidentally. Students will let you know very quickly if the mark on your records is less than the mark you wrote on their scripts!

12  **Give students responsibility.** Many colleges expect students to keep their own assessed work and to provide it on demand for external moderators and examiners. You do not have to stack all the files in your office for safe keeping.

# 29

# Giving students feedback

Students can learn a great deal from feedback from their tutors, as well as from feedback to and from each other. The following suggestions may help you to make your feedback both more useful to your students and more readily-received by your students.

1  **Make feedback timely.** Feedback should provide opportunities for personal development, and the impact of feedback is much higher when it is received while students still have, fresh in their minds, the thinking they did on the work being assessed. Too often, feedback is received by students only after a particular part of the course has been completed, and the potential benefits that they would have received if the feedback had been received earlier are reduced.

2  **Maximize your use of any whole-group sessions to explain feedback to students on work that has been assessed.** Where there have been common problems or difficulties experienced by students, it can be particularly useful for detailed explanations to be given to them at a time when they can compare their own work with that of fellow students. This can also help students who have had problems to feel that they were not the only ones to have got things wrong.

3  **Say 'well done'.** Putting ticks against things that students got right or did well is not well received. It is far more effective to say (and write) a few well-chosen words of praise. It is also important not to lose your credibility with your students by saying 'well done' in the same way too often. Think of as many different ways of confirming and reinforcing good work as you can.

4  **Save the real accolades for when they are deserved.** If you write 'splendid' beside something that was in fact quite easy for students to achieve, they will not trust your accolades in future. 'Yes, I agree' may be a more suitable message of confirmation for things that did not stretch the students.

5   **Take care when giving feedback about things that students have not done well.** It is too easy just to put red crosses or underlining against students' errors. A few carefully chosen words will often be of more value to them. They usually need to know exactly what they should have done, rather than just the fact that they were incorrect.

6   **Protect students' confidence levels.** Feedback messages along the lines of 'This was a tricky question', or 'Most people found this bit difficult', can do much to prevent students who had problems from thinking that they must be the only people in the world ever to have had such difficulties. Restrict the number of criticisms you make for the same reasons.

7   **Think about devising a feedback sheet.** When a fairly large group of students has tackled a particular piece of work, it can be economical in time and effort to compose a short handout. This will list and explain the most common difficulties that students experienced with the work. It can also be coupled usefully with a model answer or a commentary on the features that would be looked for in a good answer to the task.

8   **Consider ways of getting students to give feedback to each other.** It can be really useful to students to compare their work together, and to see the strengths and weaknesses in different ways of approaching their work on tasks. Using student peer-assessment is a way of helping students to look at each other's work in even greater detail, as well as reflecting deeply on their own attempts to do the tasks involved.

9   **Get students to self-assess their own work.** It can be useful to devise a specific self-assessment proforma for an individual piece of assessed work, and to ask students to complete this and hand it in along with their work. Feedback can then be linked to things that the students themselves know are good or bad about their attempts, as well as to areas where students may have been unaware of their strengths or weaknesses.

10  **Make feedback individual where possible.** When students have been involved in negotiating the assessment criteria to be employed when assessing their work, some of the criteria may be applied on an individual basis, as in learning agreement frameworks. Then it is particularly useful to give students individual feedback on how they have done regarding their own criteria.

11 **Ask students exactly what feedback they would appreciate (and in what format).** It is useful to do this occasionally, so that you can respond directly to the questions that individual students may have about their own attempts at particular pieces of work. Some may ask for specific feedback on things like spelling, structure or grammar, or on whether their work is directly relevant to the task as briefed. Some may appreciate a standardized proforma; others the record of a one-to-one discussion or observation.

12 **Gather feedback on your feedback.** It can be useful to find out from students how they are finding the feedback you are giving them on their work. Ask them what the most useful things are that they learn from your feedback, and what aspects of your feedback they enjoy least, too. This helps you to further tune in your feedback towards being as acceptable and useful as possible to students.

# Chapter 5    Supporting Diverse Students

This chapter looks at identifying some of the principal client groups of further and continuing education, where there may be a need to think more deeply about the particular needs of such students.

We begin with a set of suggestions and ideas which broadly describe some of the main types of students that we deal with, and some basic information about a few of the key terms and acronyms that are encountered in our work.

We move on to look at some of the particular needs of mature students. It can be a real pleasure working with mature students, not least because they are more demanding, and have often got better reasons for being on our courses than have some of their younger counterparts. However, we need to do all we can both to live up to the expectations that mature students have regarding their education and meeting their particular needs.

Next we consider separately some of the particular issues and problems that can arise when working with part-time students. This client group seems likely to continue to grow.

Then we offer some suggestions about ways of addressing some of the particular needs of international students. The proportion of these students varies considerably across disciplines and at different localities. Even when international students are in a distinct minority, it makes a great deal of difference to their learning experience (and life experience) if we take the care necessary to address some of their most specific needs and requirements.

We conclude this chapter with a set of suggestions about 'special needs' students. When writing these, we could not help feeling that some of the issues and needs we thought about were so important that there may well be room for a whole book devoted to how best to maximize the learning opportunities for these students. In the context of this book, we hope that we have prioritized their needs effectively in the suggestions that we have included.

# 30

# Constituencies and contexts of continuing and further education

Students in further and continuing education have a diverse range of needs, and the term 'continuing education' refers to a wide range of students studying for different purposes and reasons. Under this heading we outline a range of different kinds of continuing and further education student situations, and give brief explanations of some of the terms and acronyms which are most frequently encountered. At this stage, we do not offer suggestions as such on how to meet the particular needs of the various categories of students we mention, as the rest of this book provides more detailed suggestions about the teaching, learning and assessment of all of these students. Our intention in the present context is to remind you of some of the terminology in use, and the overlaps and differences between students studying in different ways.

1    **Extra-mural students.** These were traditionally adults returning to college to learn for their own self-improvement, or just for fun. Usually their study programmes consisted of lectures and sometimes practical sessions, but without formal assessment or exams. However, there has been a rapid switch of such programmes towards credit-rated modules including assessment, for example in the UK, where funding for continuing education has become dependent upon such credit-rating.

2    **Continuing professional development students on extended courses.** Such students include people in employment, studying part-time or full-time at college with support from their employers, to gain specific qualifications or competences relevant to their work, where the period of study spans months or years in overall duration.

3   **Short-course students.** These also may be studying for continuing professional development reasons, but on highly specific, skills-based programmes, maybe from one-week duration to a period spanning a term or semester, to help them pick up particular competences or qualifications. Examples range from the use of a particular computing package to finding out about new safety regulations.

4   **Further education students.** In the UK, 'further education' embraces a wide range of post-school vocational education, some of which is designed to lead into employment directly, and some of which enables students to proceed to higher education programmes.

5   **Lifelong education students.** This term spans both academic and vocational education programmes, provided by colleges or universities, where the primary intention is that education and training opportunities are available to students at different stages of their careers and lives.

6   **Access students.** This term is broadly used in the context of programmes of study provided both by universities and further education colleges, where the primary aim is to help students to proceed to higher education programmes. Access courses often address particularly the needs of students who were not qualified on leaving school to go straight into higher education, but who now wish to move in this direction.

7   **Foundation course students.** There is a strong overlap with access provision here, but foundation courses are normally designed to equip students to proceed to higher level courses in a particular institution. Many universities design and run their own foundation courses. Alternatively, colleges of further education may run these courses designed to meet the entry conditions of one or more particular universities. They often do so as part of franchising arrangements, where the universities themselves are involved in the design, quality assurance and delivery of the courses in the colleges.

8   **CATS: Credit Accumulation and Transfer Systems.** These are systems where individual elements of study bear agreed credit points, allowing students to accumulate credits through their studies in a wide variety of full-time, part-time or short-course modes, at different kinds of colleges or universities. Agreed levels of credits can allow students to proceed to the first (or a later) year of degree courses in higher education institutions.

9    **NVQs: National Vocational Qualifications.** These could be described as a particular form of credit accumulation operating in the UK (with SNVQs in Scotland), relating mainly to competence-based qualifications in vocational areas, including management and some areas of education and training. Students working towards these qualifications may do so at colleges and at some universities, but may alternatively do so in the context of their employment without necessarily attending any formal college-based courses or programmes.

10   **GNVQ (General National Vocational Qualifications) students.** These are normally 16–19 year old students, studying competence-based programmes either in schools or at further education colleges, to a curriculum agreed nationally across England and Wales. Their assessment is based on evidence they accumulate to demonstrate their achievement of given learning outcomes, by evidence that is mapped against set performance criteria and evidence indicators.

11   **APL and APEL.** These acronyms refer to the principles of the accreditation and/or assessment of prior experience and learning. Such processes are based on awarding students credit for work they have already done, on the basis of them furnishing suitable evidence of their achievements. Students may then be exempted from having to take particular options or courses as they proceed to further study.

12   **Open College Networks (OCN).** In the UK, these are collaborative partnerships between such organizations as adult education providers, local education authorities, colleges, Training and Enterprise Councils (TECs) and voluntary groups. They can assess and accredit learning programmes for adults within a national framework provided by the National Open College Network, and are recognized by the Further Education Funding Council for funding purposes. Elements of competence or achievement for adults may be accredited on the basis of evidence which they can bring forward from their prior learning or their work-based experience.

# 31

# Mature students

In further and continuing education, a common factor is that many of our students are mature, and are often returning to education after some years in employment. Indeed, some students are very mature and start learning again as a retirement pursuit. It is important that we treat mature students appropriately, and that they feel comfortable even when in groups or classes where they are working alongside much younger students. The following suggestions may alert you to some of the principal issues which arise when working with mature students, particularly when doing so in the context of courses which also include younger students.

1   **Be aware of the anxieties that mature students often have when first returning to studying.** They may have negative memories of their last experiences in education and things may have changed a great deal since they were last students. Try not to allow them to feel vulnerable or exposed until they have had sufficient time to gain confidence.

2   **Remember that mature students may know a lot.** Their work experience could well have equipped them with knowledge of how some of the topics they are studying relate to the real world, and it is worth giving them the chance to share this experience. This can do a lot to increase their confidence in the group, especially in contexts where their younger counterparts are ahead of them in other ways, such as a familiarity with computers and electronic communication.

3   **Some mature students tend to be demanding.** This is not likely to be a problem with continuing education students who are just returning to learning for fun or for personal satisfaction, but can be a serious problem with students on assessed credit-rated programmes of study. Such students often take their studying a lot more seriously than some of their younger counterparts, one reason being that they are often footing the bill themselves, or are being invested in by their employers. They also tend to return to education with the more serious attitudes that may have been prevalent when they were last in an education system. Helping them

overcome their concerns can be a major step to developing their confidence in their ability to succeed, which in turn is probably one of the most significant factors predetermining their success.

4   **Remember that mature students do not know everything – or may be 'rusty'.** Just because mature students look older does not automatically mean that they have picked up some of the things that their younger counterparts have learned. There will be gaps, so ensure that mature students find out about these gaps with minimum embarrassment. Similarly, mature students may be out of practice in some academic skills such as essay writing or notemaking. It can be useful to offer 'refresher' tips to groups of mature students before anyone reveals any such shortcomings. Specifically designed study-support, or learning skills induction programmes, for mature students can be most valuable to them and much appreciated by them.

5   **Take care about assumptions.** Some mature students will have covered ground you might never have expected them to have done, and others will not have experienced things you would have expected them to have covered. It is well worth spending a little time finding out a bit more about mature students' views of their own strengths and weaknesses.

6   **Consider designing a self-profiling questionnaire for all of your students.** This can give you an accurate picture of where the skills and competences of your mature students and their younger classmates overlap or diverge.

7   **Check out the expectations of your mature students.** Ask them why they have chosen to study your subject, and how they believe it will fit into their future careers, or how it may feed into their plans for further studying. They will often have more definite answers to these questions than younger students who are simply taking your subject because it is part of their whole course.

8   **Treat mature students appropriately.** They do not like being treated like children – but, of course, neither do younger students – or children themselves! It is worth reminding yourself that at least some mature students who are just learners in your classroom are likely to be experienced professionals like yourself in other places. Be sensitive about the different focus that mature students need regarding their first week or two on a course.

9   **Help mature students to save face.** Mature people often do not like to be seen to get things wrong, especially when seen by younger people. Watch out for occasions when feedback from assessments may raise this issue. Be sensitive to mature students' feelings when they make contributions in class; if their comments or questions are shown to be 'silly' or inappropriate, such students can take this as a serious blow to their confidence.

10  **Give mature students the chance to interact well with the rest of the group.** When choosing groups for tasks or projects, it is often worth trying to get a good mix regarding age and background, to allow exchange of knowledge and experience in as many directions as possible.

11  **Be realistic about other demands on mature students' time and energy.** They normally have abundant motivation and drive, but sometimes other pressures in their lives can affect the possibility of them meeting deadlines or targets.

12  **Be a mature student yourself.** It is always useful to put yourself in a position similar to that of your students. Even if the course or topic you are studying is a minor part of your life, being a learner again will alert you to ways of refreshing your own teaching practice. It can be particularly helpful to take an assessed course yourself, as this will remind you what it feels like to prepare yourself for a tutor to look critically at your work. This can help you remain sensitive to the feelings of your students.

13  **Suggest the formation of a Mature Students' Group.** This can provide not only moral support and social activities, but may be able to give practical help to mature students through the organization of grants, rebates and focused help on the problems most likely to be encountered by such students.

# 32

# Part-time students

Universities and colleges have experienced a major shift towards the provision of part-time courses for students, and this trend is certain to continue, with greater numbers of people requiring professional updating programmes and mid-career retraining. The majority of continuing education programmes, or continuing professional development courses, are offered on a part-time basis. However, it is becoming more common to run courses and classes concurrently for both part-time and full-time students, and the following suggestions should help to ensure that the quality of provision for part-timers is enhanced even when they are studying alongside full-time students. We recognize, however, that some of the issues described below may well be beyond the direct control of further education lecturers, who may themselves experience some of the problems we mention, particularly if they are on part-time contracts themselves.

1   **Remember that part-time students are not full-time students.** In particular, they have not got the time to spend on unproductive activities such as waiting around, queuing, sorting out administrative details and other things that can be done easily by full-time students in between classes and lectures. As part-time students have less chance to solve problems with course documentation by talking to each other, ensure that all written guides and instructions that they use are particularly clear and unambiguous.

2   **Part-time students often have cars.** Make provision for part-timers to have the chance to apply for restricted parking permits, such as Wednesday only. Lack of equal treatment regarding car parking often makes part-time students feel like second-class citizens even before they get to their classes. Continuing education students need to see that they have the same opportunities as full-time students.

3   **Take into account childcare responsibilities.** Even when part-time students have high motivation and ability, those with such responsibilities may be quite unable to guarantee to attend any session if needed urgently elsewhere. It is therefore particularly important that when such students miss important sessions for good reasons, every effort needs to be made to help them catch up.

4   **Think carefully about the starting-time for part-time sessions.** When classes for part-timers start at 10.00, it may be impossible for them to find anywhere to park their cars, as everywhere will already be full. Coming in at 08.20 to park means wasting a lot of their precious time, or if they call in at their workplace before coming to college they may well be delayed or prevented from coming altogether by pressing demands. Consider timing the start of part-time sessions early, and even *before* normal full-time classes commence for part-time students without caring responsibilities.

5   **Have special library arrangements to suit part-timers.** This can include arranging priority status for short loans on selected key texts for part-time students, and library hours that allow them to come in after work or at weekends.

6   **Make face-to-face time as relevant as possible for part-time students.** In particular, make sure that they are not sitting passively listening to things they already know. Check out at the beginning of each topic to find out what the existing knowledge base is in the group and prioritize your agenda accordingly. Use face-to-face time for things where part-timers really need a shared experience. Part-time students have less opportunity to talk to each other than full-timers, and we need to make sure that they get as much feedback from each other as we can arrange during the times the group is together.

7   **Choose the topics well for class sessions.** Use valuable contact time to address subjects where part-timers are likely to need your expertise. This means choosing to spotlight important parts of the syllabus, and dealing with these in depth, rather than trying to run through the whole syllabus during limited contact time.

8   **Make it easy for part-timers to work on their own through appropriate parts of the syllabus.** Turn notes, handouts, and other learning resources into effective self-study materials, so that part-timers can make their own way through topics that do not normally cause problems. Consider the potential benefits of making study materials and tutor comment available to part-time students by e-mail.

9   **Making video recordings of key lectures, seminars or tutorials can be a real benefit to part-time students.** When they miss a session unavoidably, they can catch up very significantly if it is possible for them to see exactly what they missed. It is, therefore, worth considering making sure that there is an alternative way for part-timers to capture particularly important course sessions.

10 **Don't assume that part-time students have out-of-hours access to facilities.** All of their in-college time is likely to be timetabled in classes. If they require information technology facilities for work to be handed in for assessment, they may need a longer lead-in time to allow them to arrange access to such facilities.

11 **Lack of refreshments provision can be a real problem.** Many part-timers arrive on campus after a busy time at their workplace, and without having had the chance to get anything to eat or drink. When campus facilities offer only limited provision, part-timers can end up hungry and dehydrated – not the best state to learn effectively. Moreover, good catering provision helps part-timers to congregate together and talk before or after sessions, and the learning payoff of such interaction is highly significant.

12 **Part-time students may need the same sorts of help as full-time students.** Support services such as counselling and personal tutoring can be just as crucial for part-time as for full-time students. Problems can remain unsolved if the support provision does not extend to times when part-timers can make use of it.

13 **Take particular care regarding referred reading and set coursework.** Part-timers may not have the time to read widely, and it helps them a lot if you make references quite specific, indicating to them exactly what you intend them to derive from their work with each source. Because of the other demands on their time, part-time students need plenty of notice of deadlines for assessed coursework, and additional leeway if they are finding it hard to meet particular deadlines.

14 **Use alternative means of communication for part-timers.** Use internal mail for question-and-answer communication between yourself and part-time students, and (for those students with access to appropriate facilities) make the most of e-mail and computer conferencing possibilities. Consider having a telephone helpline, say daily from 18.30–19.30, when someone is available in the office to pick up problems and reassure students.

15 **Keep part-time students informed.** Find systems for letting them know about changes to timetables, or other changes which are often last minute ones. They hate travelling in only to find that their lecture that day has been rearranged or cancelled.

# 33

# International students

The suggestions we offer below aim to alert you to some of the particular help that may be needed by certain cross-sections of your student population. For example, students from other countries, or from a different ethnic background to the majority of your students, may need additional support in various ways, and at different stages of their studying. The suggestions below aim to help you minimize the disadvantages that such students can experience, when they are studying on programmes where they may be minority groups.

1   **Arrange specialist induction provision for international students.** Pre-sessional sessions addressing aspects of cultural acclimatization, and study-skills good practice, can be of enormous benefit in helping such students start off their academic studies without being disadvantaged

2   **Produce clear information for international students.** Try to ensure that they receive this information before they arrive at college. Ideally we should be producing clear information for all students, such as using course handbooks, but it is particularly important that international students should receive good documentation about their courses, as well as about the institution and its environs. International students are more likely to need to revisit such information again and again until they have tuned in to their new situation, and they can often do this more successfully when the information is in print rather than in easy-to-forget face-to-face formats.

3   **Help students from other countries or cultures to understand what is expected of them in assessment.** Assessment cultures vary widely around the world, and what is regarded as normal practice in some places is seen as cheating or plagiarism in others. It is important that all students are aware of the ways they are expected to behave in preparing for and undertaking any kind of assessment. It can be particularly important to help students adjust to those parts of their courses involving independent study, and about how to prepare for the assessment associated with such studies.

4    **Help them to understand what is expected of them in seminars.** Many international students come from cultures with particularly formal methods of education and find it hard to cope with the more interactive modes of teaching. Students from some cultures can find it a shock to encounter the full and frank debates between students and tutors which are regarded as healthy indicators of a seminar. This may explain their own reluctance to become involved, and they will need patient encouragement to adopt the roles that they are expected to play in their new setting.

5    **Search for ways of lessening the isolation of international students.** Encourage them out of the institution, so they can absorb more of the local culture, and make new contacts and friends, without putting them under any pressure to break their normal links with fellow students from the same background.

6    **Be sensitive on issues of religion.** Some religions require followers to pray at specific times and in particular settings. This can be a problem for students required to fit in with tight timetabling, and sensitive flexibility needs to be shown regarding their needs and rights.

7    **Help students with special food requirements.** Coping with a new culture is enough of a hurdle for students from different backgrounds and cultures, without imposing the additional burden of having to cope with 'majority' food habits. Gather feedback on what would be acceptable alternatives, that could be built into menus and catering provision. Advise those arranging catering at induction events to be especially sensitive about labelling food, so that international students do not become anxious about what they can and cannot eat.

8    **Consider getting previous students from each country to write an introductory guide to the idiosyncrasies of the British.** It can be useful for new students from overseas, and for staff and students not from abroad, to get the chance to see themselves through the eyes of people from other countries.

9    **Recognize cultural differences regarding attitudes to alcohol.** Even if mainstream attitudes are alcohol tolerant, significant groups of staff and students come from cultures where alcohol may be forbidden on religious grounds. Sensitivity regarding attitudes to alcohol does not just mean expecting groups of students, whatever their background, to go on field trips or visits which include a stop on the way back at a suitable pub. Class discussions of alcohol marketing strategies or pub social behaviours will be offensive or alien to students (or staff) whose culture forbids alcohol.

10   **Consider the special facilities needed by students from other countries.**
For example, toilet and washing facilities need to accommodate the
different practices that are involved in some cultures or religions. When
such students attempt to make use of 'normal' facilities, their actions are
in danger of being misunderstood.

11   **Consider the accommodation needs of students from other cultures.**
Students from some countries, when booking their place at university in
the UK, may not know what is meant by 'hall of residence', 'single-study-
bedroom' or 'shared student apartment'. Accommodation literature needs
to be written or supplemented so that all students know what each
category of accommodation entails.

12   **Offer language support at appropriate levels.** Students studying in
English as a second or other language will need different sorts of language
support as they continue their studies. At first, they may need help in
getting started in English, but later the help they need may be more
connected to how they should use written language in assessed work,
and spoken English in interviews with tutors or in oral examinations.

13   **Help them to communicate with home, especially in emergencies.**
International telephone or fax charges are high, and students may not
have access to locations where they can use such communications in
relative privacy. The costs, both financial and academic, of students having
to make emergency visits home are more serious, and ways need to be
found of helping students to sort out some of the problems that could
lead them into such costs.

14   **Make arrangements to celebrate success.** Students who come to study
from other countries are often unable to celebrate their achievements at
the times when their results are available, by which time they may have
gone home. Consider having end-of-teaching-session events as well as,
or instead of, end-of-course events.

# 34

# Supporting students with special needs

Colleges have a responsibility to provide the best possible educational opportunities within their remit for all students. Open-access policies, together with statutory requirements, mean that we need to take into account the requirements of students with special needs when planning our programmes of learning. These suggestions are designed to help you think about how best to approach this.

1   **Adopt a positive action approach.** Students with special needs should not be regarded as a problem to be dealt with, rather as a constituency of users whose needs must be taken into account, as the UK FECS report on 'Inclusive Learning' recommends.

2   **Involve the students in managing the support you offer.** The people who are most affected are usually the best to advise you on appropriate support strategies. They should be consulted alongside specialist external advisers when designing your provision.

3   **Think carefully about the language you use.** The term 'handicapped' can cause offence, since it is derived from those who came 'cap in hand' to ask for help. 'Disability' can also be seen as a derogatory term, suggesting something of less value than ability. People with special needs usually prefer to be regarded as people first and last, rather than being categorized by what they cannot do.

4   **Don't assume that people with mobility problems are wheelchair-bound.** Most people entitled to use the UK orange badge on their vehicles are not, in fact, users of wheelchairs. They may, however, experience difficulties in walking long distances, climbing stairs or undertaking other strenuous activities. Be aware of hidden disabilities, such as asthma and heart problems.

5 **Don't use difficult buildings as an excuse to exclude people with special needs.** It can be expensive and difficult to install lifts, automatic doors and ramps, especially into old buildings, but lateral thinking can work wonders. Careful timetabling can permit the teaching of classes, including someone with mobility problems, in ground-floor or easy-access rooms. In the UK, government funds are often available to improve access when a need has been clearly identified.

6 **Help people with visual impairments.** Colleges can do much to help students who do not see well, to study effectively. Allowing students to tape-record classes, and making available on loan recording equipment from the college, can help considerably. Visual impairment is frequently not total, and lecturers can do their bit by using large font sizes on overhead transparencies, and making material available to students who find it difficult to copy from the board or screen in class. The mobility of people with visual impairments can be improved moderately easily by such means as Braille signing, tactile strips on corridor floors, and 'talking' lifts.

7 **Help students which hearing difficulties.** Many colleges now have audio loop systems which enable students to amplify sound in classrooms. These can be supplemented by individual lecturers ensuring that students who do not hear well can have their choice of seats in class, to best facilitate audibility, by speaking clearly, and by providing back-up material on request.

8 **Make provision for students with learning difficulties.** These students cope well in colleges, especially when given additional targeted support as required in the classroom and around the college, and can fully contribute to the life of the institution. Learning resources centres can be especially helpful in providing a range of resources to support the learning of these students.

9 **Provide support for students with, and recovering from, mental illness.** Individual counselling and guidance can be enormously beneficial in enabling these students to use college study as part of a programme of personal recovery and development.

10 **Keep in mind health and safety requirements for students with special needs.** Procedures for fire or bomb threat evacuation need to take account of those people who cannot move fast, may not hear or see warnings, or who may be unduly alarmed by emergency situations. Ensure that your strategies for coping with emergencies of all kinds take account of the special needs of all of your students.

11    **Seek out additional support.** In the UK, the Further Education Funding Council provides funding for individuals to have helpers who can take notes, wordprocess assignments, sign and lip read in class to help students. This funding can also cover the purchase of specialist equipment.

# Chapter 6   Managing Your Professional Life

So far we have mostly concentrated on suggestions that are related to the optimum learning experience (and fair assessment) of your students. In this chapter we turn our attention more directly to the intended readers of this book – such as you!

We begin with some suggestions about 'Managing your time'. Probably you have already attended time-management courses, but somehow there never seems to be the time to put into practice the undoubtedly good advice that these courses contain. We hope that our practical suggestions lend themselves better to your own busy life and workload.

We move on to 'Dealing with stress'. It would be unwise to hide from the reality that many colleagues find themselves in work situations that produce considerable levels of stress, and it is our intention to confront some of the issues that cause such stress. This leads directly into 'Coping with the effects of change', which is one of the most significant causes of stress to many colleagues in further and continuing education today.

We follow these suggestions with some directly geared towards 'Looking after yourself', where we offer some tips to help you keep your professional life in a realistic position in relation to your whole life.

'Coping with heavier workloads' is also part of this picture, and here we hope to offer you some practical steps towards ensuring that you are not swamped by the demands of your profession.

Next we look at one of the factors that can cause stress and overload – that of preparing for an impending merger between your own institution and another.

'Being an effective colleague' looks at some of the ways that you as an individual can help to offset some of the stresses and strains that are affecting further education colleges at the present time.

Personal and professional development is not just a luxury, it is a necessity in a healthy profession, and our suggestions on this are intended to encourage you to make it an important part of your working life.

We continue with a set of suggestions directly addressed to colleagues who are part-time lecturers. They sometimes find themselves feeling all of the strains, yet deriving only some of the benefits associated with the profession they have joined. In England, the Report of the Quality Assessment Committee of the Further Education Funding Council (Circular 97/20) noted that the increased proportion of part-time lecturers brings more up to date experience of commerce and industry to the sector, and benefits students, and at the same time the greater use of casual workforce reduces costs. However, the Report also noted that part-time staff rarely engage in curriculum development, student support and guidance activities, extra-curricular activities, formal staff appraisal or in-service training. Our suggestions for part-time staff represent a starting point from which to move towards addressing these problems. We end this chapter with some suggestions about how to ensure that your contract of employment is a reasonable basis for your professional career.

# 35

# Managing your time

How much time can be managed is open to question. Often further education lecturers have much of their time predetermined by line managers and teaching timetables. But even if only a quarter or third of your working time is under your control, we feel the following tips will help you to make it more productive.

1  **Budget your time.** Your 'budget' is that time in your working day that is not predetermined by your teaching timetable and any other requirements of your managers. To budget effectively, you will need to tackle tasks systematically rather than trying to do everything at once.

2  **Keep a list of the work you need to do under a series of headings.** These headings could make up a priority list of: *must do immediately; should do soon; may be put on the back-burner;* or reflect a four-way split of each item of work as *urgent and complex or important; urgent but routine; complex or important but not urgent; routine and not urgent.* This task list is best drawn up on a daily basis, crossing out or carrying forward items as you tackle them.

3  **Avoid the temptation to do the routine and not urgent tasks first.** They tempt because they can be simple, distracting or even fun. But keep a note of them; they can be done in the quieter patches. However, there are benefits to be gained from spending up to half an hour on a non-urgent task before starting on an urgent one.

4  **Whichever list you use, remember it is dynamic and will need to be reviewed daily**. Time has a nasty habit of moving things on and what was once not urgent emerges suddenly as something needed yesterday. Remember too that you may be better off by doing three things from your list in part rather than spending all your time budget on just one of them.

5   **Use a wall chart or a 'What am I doing?' grid.** Such devices provide you with a means to plan ahead and schedule your known commitments. They also tell other people about your current activities. It is useful for your colleagues if you also include a location and a note of how you may be contacted.

6   **Keep your paperwork well filed**. It is a temptation just to 'pile' the in, out and pending trays. Do this and you will inevitably spend ages looking for that vital piece of information or, in despair, assume that it has been lost (or not received). Use a relatively quiet time to set up, maintain, and update your filing system.

7   **Is your journey really necessary?** Avoid multiple trips to the photocopier or mail point. Ask yourself: 'Rather than see someone, would it be quicker to phone, e-mail or write?' 'Do I really need to go to such-and-such meeting?' 'Do I actually need to go to the *whole* of that meeting?'

8   **Work out which tasks you can delegate and do so**. Even with tight staffing levels, there will be clerical and technical support staff. Often such staff are better able than you to do the routine jobs like typing, filing, or photocopying. They can be quicker, too. Junior colleagues may be pleased to help with administrative functions as a way to help them develop their skills or 'visibility' in your organization.

9.  **Each day schedule particular times to make your phone calls and to check your e-mail**. Making and receiving calls and e-mails *ad hoc* across the working day can be time wasting and distracting from other tasks. Invest in an 'ansaphone' or 'voice mail' as a way to control but not to lose calls. Encourage those you phone, but never seem to be available, to invest in similar technology.

10  **Try the *do it now* technique**. Do not be put off if you cannot do the whole task in one bite. Break it up into smaller components that you can and will do straight away. You can eat an elephant, if you nibble a bit at a time!

11  **In the end you must decide what kinds of activity have a high pay-off or a low pay-off for you in terms of your time investment**. You may find that, for you, doing your paperwork by e-mail and phoning rather than writing will have high pay-offs. And you might find that attending meetings has a low pay-off, as may be writing jobs-to-do lists.

# 36

# Dealing with stress

Working in further education can be extremely stressful as staff are put under increasing pressure to teach longer hours and in possibly unfamiliar ways, and to spend longer hours on assessment and record keeping. At the same time, students are becoming more diverse and have an ever widening range of requirements and expectations. Behind this is a service that is under increasing pressure to deliver more with less. These tips cannot eliminate your stress, but may be able to suggest some strategies to help you deal with it.

1   **Don't ignore stress.** There are no prizes for struggling to the point of collapse: indeed, this is the last thing you should be doing. As the symptoms of stress become apparent to you, such as sleep disturbances, eating problems, weight gain or loss, headaches or just finding you are on an increasingly short fuse, try to identify the causes of your stress and do something about it.

2   **Allow yourself to feel anger.** It is not surprising that people under stress often feel full of rage, which is often not specifically directed. People often become very frustrated when they feel powerless, so it may be worth taking stock of what is and what is not within your control. Anger, once generated, can be directed in many directions, and the most harmful of these is inwards. All the same, it is unwise, as well as unprofessional, to vent your rage on others, especially innocent bystanders who are caught in the cross-fire. Find ways to let off steam that are not destructive to yourself and others. These may include some vigorous gardening or other exercise (within your own capabilities), a long walk or even smashing a few plates!

3   **Write it out of your system.** Some people find it very helpful to write about the issues that stress them and make them angry. This can take the form of a diary in which you record your feelings and analyse the situation, or letters you would like to send to the people who are causing you stress,

or use other forms of escapist or academic writing to take your mind off the current situation. Be very careful, however, about the ways in which you use your writing. Try to avoid firing off missives in anger that you might regret at a later stage.

4   **Have some fun.** Look for ways in which you can de-stress yourself by doing things that make you happy. A little hedonism goes a long way. Think about the things that give you pleasure like cooking, reading for pleasure, going to concerts or having a day of total sloth. Regard these as part of a programme of active stress management rather than as a guilt-inducing interference with your work. You deserve some time for yourself and you should not regard it as a luxury.

5   **Don't be afraid to go to the doctor.** The worst excesses of stress can be helped by short term medication and medical intervention of some kind. People are often unwilling to resort to a visit to their GP for matters of stress when they would not hesitate to seek help for a physical ailment. Do not let such feelings get in the way of finding the kind of support you need.

6   **Try not to worry about not sleeping.** Sleep disturbance is one of the most common features of stress and worrying about it makes it worse. Try to ensure that you are warm and comfortable at bedtime, avoid working for at least an hour before you retire and use music or reading to help get you into a relaxed state. If sleep does not come, try to use the rest period to recoup some energy and try not to go over in your mind what is troubling you. Many people fail to recognize that they need less sleep as they get older, and it is unrealistic to expect always to get seven or eight unbroken hours. Make the most of cat naps and snoozes when you can, and try not to let anxiety about lack of sleep exacerbate the problem. Taking exercise and cutting down on your caffeine intake can also help.

7   **Use relaxation techniques.** There are innumerable methods that can be used to help you unwind, including deep breathing, massage, aromatherapy and meditation. It might be worth your while to explore the techniques that sound most attractive to you and try to use them to help you cope with stress.

8   **Work it out in the gym.** It may feel like the last thing on earth you want to do is to take physical exercise at the end of a long stressful day, but lots of people find it helps them relax. Join a gym, take the dog for long walks, swim, take up golf, play a mean game of squash or just do aerobics at home to help your body to become as tired physically as your mind is mentally. Find out what type of exercise works best for you and try to use

it as a bridge between your working life and your own time. The time you spend will be a sound investment in helping you keep on top (but try not to let your exercise requirement end up feeling like another kind of work you have to do).

9  **Get a life outside college.** Family and friends still deserve your attention, even if work is very busy, and we all need to learn to keep a sense of proportion to our lives. Try not to neglect hobbies and interests, even if you sleep through the film or nod off after the sweet course. Let your pets help you to remember how to be a human, too.

10  **Take a break.** Often our panics over time management are caused not so much by how much we have to do as by whether we feel we have sufficient time to do it in. Try to take a real break from time to time, so as to help you get your workload into proportion. A little holiday or a whole weekend without college work occasionally can make you better able to cope with the onslaught on your return.

11  **Prioritize your tasks.** Try to sort your work into jobs that are urgent or not and important or not. Do urgent, important things first and do them well; do urgent unimportant things soon too, but do not spend too much time on them. You will have a great glow of achievement about having got them out of the way. Block in time for the important, non-urgent tasks, so you can do them most effectively. Review carefully the jobs you think are neither important nor urgent and either put them in a basket of work to do when you have a minute or are bored with your more immediate tasks, or throw them away.

12  **Overcome powerlessness with action.** When you are stressed out, it is often because you feel totally powerless in the situation. It can be useful to look at the areas you do have some control over and try to do something about them, however minor. This may not change the overall picture very much, but will probably make you feel better.

13  **Talk about your problems.** Actually voicing what is stressing you to a colleague, a line manager, the person you are closest too or even your cat can sometimes improve the situation. Bottling it all up through some misplaced sense of fortitude can be dangerous.

14  **Try counselling.** Many colleges have someone to whom staff can turn for trained counselling in times of great stress. Otherwise you could look elsewhere through your GP or in the phone book under therapeutic practice or alternative medicine to find someone who can guide and

support you through the worst patches. This is often more productive than piling all your stress onto your nearest and dearest who usually have problems of their own.

15 **Separate the personal from the professional.** A lot of what is happening in further education is about structures and processes rather than individual people. Try, if you can, not to see what is being done as a personal attack on you.

16 **Try not to personalize the situation into hatred and blame.** It is easy to fall into the trap of seeing all your stress as being caused by an individual or group of people who have it in for you. Of course it may be the case, but usually high stress situations are caused by cockup rather than conspiracy.

17 **Avoid compounding the problem.** If things are very stressful at work, try to avoid making important life changes at the same time, such as moving to a larger house or starting a family, if these can be deferred for a while.

18 **Audit your intake of stimulants.** For those whose culture allows alcohol, a little can be felt to be a wonderful relaxant, but excessive intakes can be problematic. It is natural to drink a lot of beverages containing caffeine when trying to get through a lot of work, but it can interfere with your metabolism and sleep patterns. Eating rich food too late at night and smoking too much can also get in the way of being calm. Moderation is boring but a good policy for those under stress.

19 **Try to adopt a long term perspective.** It can be really hard to project into the future and to review current stress as part of a much larger pattern, but if you can do it, it helps. Much of what seems really important now will pale into insignificance in a few weeks', months' or years' time.

20 **A problem shared is a problem doubled!** Stressed people meeting in groups can reinforce each other's stress by constantly rehearsing the problems. Encourage the group to agree a moratorium from time to time on chewing over the same old issues. Maybe have a meal out as a group or go to the races together instead. It will not take away the stress, but it might help you forget about it for a while.

# 37

# Coping with the effects of change

Further education is currently experiencing unprecedented change. There is plenty of advice on managing change, usually addressed to those whose job it is to implement change effectively. There is relatively little on coping with the effects that change brings to 'rank and file' teaching staff. Staff often feel threatened and disempowered by changes – not least those related to the impact of information technology on teaching learning and assessment. This set of tips is a modest first attempt at redressing the balance, by providing suggestions for those most affected by change.

1   **Try to see change as a positive opportunity.** Many people instinctively react against change. This is quite normal. It is equally natural that change is always happening and never stops. The alternative to change is often stagnation, leading to the ultimate failure of your organization. Remember that there are usually compelling reasons for initiating change. These may include the implementation of a new curriculum or a different financial regime. Resisting change is ultimately futile: look for more effective ways to react. It can be useful to identify opportunities for staff development or to learn new skills.

2   **Recognize that change can make you feel unsettled and confused**. Do not take it as a personal attack on you, your job or your field of expertise. Often such change is depersonalized and driven by organizational and financial factors.

3   **Try to make some kind of investment in the change**. You (as an individual) will not be able to prevent the change from taking place, but you will be better able to influence its implementation and modify its effects. It may make you feel better too.

4   **Try to get hold of accurate, up to date and full information.** It is too easy for gossip, the local grapevine and even deliberate misinformation to gain currency, making an uncertain situation even worse. Your organization may not be as open as you would wish, but accurate information will usually be available through your staff representatives, managers or administrators.

5   **Network, network and network**. People in the midst of change need the support of others within the same situation, and of those outside of it. Everyone benefits from the exchange of (accurate) information, and making joint proposals and representations to managers. Networking can also be great for simply having a good moan, but do not let that dominate proceedings, or else you will end up even more depressed.

6   **Look after yourself**. Enforced change can often make you feel powerless, so you may need to take steps to ensure that negativity does not get out of hand. Use leisure time and home pursuits to help take your mind off the current problems. Without taxing the patience of friends or family, keep them informed so that they, in turn, can help you keep a sense of proportion.

7   **Try to adopt a long-term perspective**. It is easy to be so wrapped up in the immediate issues that you lose sight of potential longer term benefits of the change for you as an individual. Use distancing techniques to help you to step back from current discomfort to explore likely future outcomes.

8   **Avoid 'downward spiralling', where everyone makes each other even more fed-up.** Try to keep away from the Cassandra and 'Moaning Minnies' within your organization. Such people make a bad situation feel like a disaster and make everyone feel demoralized.

9   **Review the scale of the changes as they affect *you*.** Allow yourself to be selfish for a moment and consider your own situation. It is not always the case that you will have to make a significant change in your own position, such as having to do something completely different or make changes to your lifestyle.

10  **Accept that there are several processes at work in your reaction to change.** You are likely to experience a sequence of denial, resistance and exploration before you can feel commitment to the change. Resist the temptation to opt out or quit. If you can be objective about what stage you have reached in this sequence, you may be able to progress more quickly and comfortably.

# 38

# Looking after yourself

A lot of this book is about surviving well in further education. Here we look specifically at your own well being. The suggestions below are tried and tested, but we expect you will find some of more use to you than others, and no doubt you will have found additional ways of looking after yourself that work for you.

1   **Know your job description.** As new tasks are added to your list of duties, keep your eye open for anything that you no longer need to do, or which can be negotiated out of your job description. It is easy for someone who has been in post for a while to end up accumulating too many jobs and roles. Use the opportunity of your staff review to have your job description altered.

2   **Remind yourself about what attracted you to your job in the first place.** Further education lecturers should not expect attractive salaries and long holidays, but the job can still be stimulating and rewarding, with opportunities for a varied working life which is rarely boring.

3   **Manage your marking.** Marking students' work can be the bane of the further education lecturer's life. When you can, schedule heavy marking loads with your different student groups, so they do not all come at once. Explore activities that can be self- or peer-graded, or that can be assessed in class, or that only require formative feedback, or that can be assessed using the computer, to supplement your traditional tutor-marking. Further suggestions on ways of handling marking loads are included in Chapter 4 on Assessment.

4   **Be realistic about taking work home.** Few further education staff will be able to get by without taking some work home, but there has to be a happy medium between having a completely clear private life and total invasion of your home life by college work.

5   **Make space for your own learning.** As a further education lecturer, you will need to update continually your knowledge, skills and competences. Think about trying to fit in working towards higher qualifications, research, and professional updating, to help you keep on top of the job. Use the opportunity of your staff review to seek support for your own learning.

6   **Use your networks.** Make use of specialist subject groupings in your field, or within your own college, or beyond, to help you keep abreast of your subject, and to give you a frame of reference about how other colleagues are looking after themselves in circumstances similar to your own.

7   **Recognize and use your strengths.** Work out how best you can contribute to the work of the team, stretching yourself at the same time, so that you can grow in the process. Again, use the opportunity of your staff review to seek new opportunities.

8   **Be aware and accepting about your weaknesses.** Recognize them, and work towards doing something about them. There will always be times when you do not feel on top of a situation. Here a trusted colleague or mentor can be used to help you work on it. Once you have diagnosed a weakness, you can identify opportunities to become better informed, better trained and even more competent.

9   **Keep learning about teaching.** This can help you look after yourself by approaching your work more efficiently and with a wider range of techniques. Attend, when you can, workshops or conferences on new or different teaching methods and on diversifying assessment. You could gain ideas that will make your life easier or more interesting. Try to keep up to date with the literature on teaching and learning, not so much scholarly pedagogic research, but the more accessible magazines and journals, which can be rich sources of ideas.

10  **Keep abreast of information technology developments.** You will need to participate in training programmes to keep pace with the rapid changes in the use of information technology in teaching and learning. It is important to be able to encourage students to use CD-ROM resources, e-mail and the Internet, and many students already come to college with well developed skills in these areas.

11  **Become an 'active enquirer'.** Learn to understand the context in which you work as this will help to empower you and reduce your stress levels. Use active enquiry techniques to help you to diagnose problems, suggest solutions, and to identify new and original approaches you can adapt to your work.

12 **Evaluate your own performance.** It is always useful to have measures of your own effectiveness ready for your staff review and also for promotion interviews. If you do not ask questions about your effectiveness, you will not get a clear picture of how you are doing. Ask everyone you can, including your students, peers, managers and (not least) yourself.

13 **Celebrate your achievements.** Keep a plaudits file in which you can place positive feedback comments on your teaching from students, parents and people who are grateful for your support, and any other indications you receive of people's approval.

14 **Collect evidence of what you have done.** Keep records of work undertaken, additional tasks you have tackled, working groups you have participated in, resources you have designed, piloted or distributed, contributions to conferences, summaries of student feedback and activity logs. Keep these, and anything else which might come in handy at a later stage, when you may need to make your case for promotion, or may be required to justify your actions if they have been called into question.

15 **Get involved in interesting new developments.** Join committees and task groups on issues in which you are interested. This will enable you to have some influence on events, increase your profile and allow you to have some ownership of changing and emerging situations.

16 **Let the curriculum inform what you do.** In further education, trends are away from didactic means of course delivery and toward student-centred learning. It will not help you if you continually hark back to the 'good old days'. Instead, go with the flow and move with the times in terms of the focus of your activities. Accept that resource-based learning, information technology and the demise of 'chalk and talk' are facts of life.

17 **Manage staff–student relationships.** It is difficult to establish and maintain appropriate boundaries, particularly when students may be very needy. Try not to allow your genuine desire to help individual students to lead you to unreasonable demands on your time.

18 **Be aware of what you can, and cannot, deal with in the way of medical emergencies.** It is not a bad idea to get some first-aid training. Most colleges will have policies about who can or should do what when students collapse or have fits, or experience traumas or accidents. Make sure you know what the policy is, who the trained staff are, and sort out for yourself what you are able to do.

19 **Don't leave yourself open to charges of harassment.** Be careful about meetings with students of either sex when the college is deserted. Avoid making jokes or friendly suggestions that could be misinterpreted. Be careful about body contact of any kind.

20 **Don't put yourself in hazardous situations.** It is still rare for a further education lecturer to be placed in violent or threatening circumstances, but such events do occur. Think about what you would do if it were to happen to you. What are the local procedures for summoning help? How would you get out? What kinds of barriers could you put between yourself and a potentially violent person?

21 **Practise indiscriminate acts of kindness, and selfless acts of thoughtfulness.** Such things will make you feel better, and lead to a better working atmosphere all round.

# 39

# Coping with heavier workloads

Heavier workloads have become a fact of life for most lecturers in further education colleges. It seems highly unlikely that this situation will change. Most countries are spending less on education and training than the UK, and the trend remains towards students themselves finding the money to fund their own education. While the authors of this book in no way believe that spending on education should be downgraded, we would like to offer readers some suggestions on how they may accommodate some of the effects of the changes.

1   **Don't waste energy on trying to turn the clock back.** What some people affectionately refer to as 'the good old days' are very unlikely to return. One danger is that we spend so much time talking about how much better things once were, that we put even more pressure on the time and energy we have to face today and plan for tomorrow.

2   **Prioritize your own workload.** It is useful to go through all the tasks and roles that you undertake, asking yourself which are the *really* important ones, and which are the ones that would not have significant effects on your students if you were to prune or abandon them.

3   **Manage your time.** When snowed under with work, the danger is that time seems to manage you. It can be worthwhile spending a couple of hours on a time management training programme. Look for that one good idea that will save you a couple of hours, again and again.

4   **Cut your assessment workload.** This does not mean reducing the quality of your assessment. Nor is it true that there is little you can do about your workload because of externally applied requirements, such as those associated with GNVQ. It is widely recognized that over-assessment is bad for students, and in former times it was all too easy for such patterns of over-assessment to be established. Now may be the time to think again about how much assessment your students really need, and to improve

the quality of this, but at the same time significantly reduce its volume. In Chapter 4 on Assessment, we provide many ideas for you to choose from about ways of doing this.

5   **Make good use of learning resource materials.** Students nowadays learn a great deal more from computer-based and print-based materials than once was the case. The quality of learning resource materials is improving all the time, and such materials are getting steadily better at giving students opportunities to learn-by-doing, and to learn from healthy trial-and-error. Materials are getting much better at providing students with feedback on their individual progress and performance. Making the most of such materials can free up valuable face-to-face time with students, so you can deal with their questions and problems rather than merely imparting information to them.

6   **Make better use of your learning centres.** Arranging for your students to do relevant parts of their learning in such centres can bring variety to their learning environment, and can relieve you of some of the responsibility for looking after them.

7   **Make good use of your administrative and support staff.** It is easy for us to find ourselves doing tasks which they could have done just as well, and probably more efficiently than ourselves.

8   **Make better use of feedback from students.** Listen to their concerns, and focus on them, making your own work more useful to them at the same time. They know better than anyone else where their problems lie, so it is worth making sure that your valuable time is spent addressing the right problems.

9   **Cut your administrative workload.** Life may seem to be full of meetings and paperwork, but is it all really necessary? A well-chaired one-hour meeting can usually achieve as much as a much longer one. Later in this book we suggest a whole set of strategies for reducing the burden associated with paperwork.

10  **Don't carry your entire workload in your mind.** We can only do one thing at a time, so when doing important work such as teaching and assessing students, do not get sidetracked into worrying about the numerous other tasks jostling for your attention. Of course, if you are already adept at multi-tasking, you do not need any advice here.

11    **Remind yourself of the things you really like about your job.** Some of the aspects may have gone now, but there will be many other things that continue to apply. Celebrate *your* learners' progress and achievement.

12    **Give yourself a break!** We have mentioned this already, but it is important enough to repeat. One of the symptoms displayed by people under pressure of work is that they seem to forget that we all need time off, and the world will not grind to a halt if we do not do everything on our 'to do' lists. Having a break, and switching your mind away entirely from the pressures, will mean you can return to the fray re-energized and strengthened.

# 40

# Coping well with mergers

In education systems suffering from reduced funding or diminishing levels of resources, mergers are seen as a way of achieving increased cost-effectiveness, and providing institutions with greater flexibility and resilience. However, mergers are necessarily preceded by a period of stress and uncertainty, and followed by a time which may necessitate considerable readjustments. The following suggestions are primarily intended to help you anticipate any potential mergers in a constructive way.

1   **Don't pretend that it is never going to happen.** There are more rumours of mergers than actual mergers, and it can be tempting to imagine that it is not going to come to anything. That said, it is sensible not to make the possibility of a merger take over your whole work, at least until it is more of a certainty than a rumour.

2   **Find out all you can about the different academic tribes involved.** Whenever two or more institutions are merged, the history and culture of the groupings that went before are vital factors in shaping what happens next. It is easier to understand and live with what is happening if you gain an understanding of the various perspectives of those involved.

3   **Be prepared for there to be winners and losers.** By their nature mergers tend only to go ahead where there are clear benefits in terms of increased market and reduced competition at minimum liability or risk for the merged organization. It is very rare for mergers to be win–win situations for all concerned. The art for the individual is to look for ways to maximize the potential for personal benefit, and to find ways of reducing the negative aspects.

4   **Accept that there will be some loss of identity.** In a merger, you need to recognize that it will be impossible for everyone to carry on just as they did previously with the historic traditions of each group remaining untouched. It is worth looking for good compromises. Reserve your battles for the important and essential qualities that you believe characterized your old situation, rather than the warm bath of the familiar.

5   **Make space for feelings.** It is often extremely painful and threatening to be involved in a merger situation. Institutions and individuals who ignore this, do so at their peril.

6   **Look for the positive in the merger.** There can be both personal and community gains from the event. Try to identify them and celebrate their realization.

7   **Don't get angry, get active.** Involve yourself in the merger process as far as possible, rather than sticking your head in the sand, so that you are likely to be able to affect the decisions that are being made, rather than being left out in the cold.

8   **Put yourself around**. Attend all the meetings that you can so that people get to know you and you have a chance to meet key people who will be involved in the newly merged organization. You can judge much more from meeting, seeing and hearing people than you can from just reading about the events.

9   **Identify kindred spirits in the organization with which you will be merging.** Actively court them and set up your own collaborative networking activities. If you can find people with whom you can identify and work, you are likely to be able to keep each other informed about what is happening from where you stand.

10  **Share paperwork with your about-to-be partners.** This way both sides can start to understand each other's contexts and mores. It is worth recognizing that handbooks often only tell half the story and there can be discontinuities between what is written and what actually happens, so the paperwork is only a starting point.

# *41*

# Being an effective colleague

Working in college can be really miserable if the people around you are not supportive and helpful. Try to start by ensuring that the people around you find you a helpful and supportive colleague, and you may be delighted at how the condition can spread.

1  **Help out when the going gets tough.** If someone in your team is struggling, it makes a big difference if you are prepared to roll up your sleeves and lend a hand, whether it is in collating marks, stuffing envelopes or preparing for an important event. With luck, they will reciprocate when you are having a tough time, too.

2  **Don't spring surprises on colleagues unnecessarily.** If you know you are going to be away for an extended period, or if you cannot fulfil your obligations, try to give as much advance notice as possible. This will enable colleagues who have to fill in the gaps for you to build them into their own schedules.

3  **Keep to deadlines, especially when they impact on others.** If you are late doing your own marking, for example, or in putting together your section of a report, it will often affect others whose own time management will be thrown out of kilter. Try, as far as humanly possible, to do what you have said you will within the time available.

4  **Keep track of what your colleagues really appreciate in what you do.** Try to do more of these things whenever you can. It can also be worth working out what a 'terrible colleague' might be like, maybe by making a word picture of a hypothetical case, and avoiding doing the sorts of things that may be brought to mind by such a picture.

5   **Find out how colleagues feel.** Do not just wait for them to tell you how they feel, and do not keep informal conversations to work-based topics. Simply asking 'how are you feeling today?' or 'what's on top for you just now?' can be open ended questions which allow colleagues to share with you things that are important to them at the time, but which would just not have arisen in normal work-oriented discussions.

6   **Be considerate when sharing an office.** Often college staff workrooms are extremely cramped for space, and colleagues who leave papers all over a shared desk and who hog all available storage space make life difficult for others. Do not leave dirty cups around, clear up your own mess, do not smoke in areas where it is not permitted and be thoughtful about noise. If students need to be seen privately, try to agree times when fellow tutors can have uninterrupted use of the space.

7   **Be punctual for meetings.** Everyone slips sometimes, for very good reasons, but as a rule, try to ensure you are always punctual for meetings, so other people are not kept waiting for you while you make a last minute phone call or a cup of tea.

8   **Keep colleagues informed about what you are doing.** People need to know what you are up to when this impacts on their work. If, for example, you know you will be filling the office with a lot of bulky portfolios to mark, it might be a good idea to tell colleagues before they fall over the boxes coming into the room. Tell them also when you will have visitors, when you will be away and when you expect to have a lot of students visiting you.

9   **Be gracious when rooms are double-booked.** This inevitably happens from time to time in colleges and can be the cause of much disagreement. Colleagues, with two or more groups of students needing to use the same room, should tackle the problem together, rather than having a slanging match over who had booked the room first. It makes sense for the group *in situ*, or the largest group, to occupy the available room with their tutor, while the other group is asked to wait somewhere like the refectory or quietly in the corridor until another room is found.

10  **Leave teaching spaces as you found them (or better).** If you move furniture or use the walls for display, try to leave the room fit for use by others when you leave. Encourage students to clear their own litter and leave the space tidy.

# 42

# Personal development and review forums

It is now a well established quality assurance measure to involve all staff in a periodic review process. This enables staff, in discussion with their line managers, to appraise the effectiveness of their performance and to consider how best to undertake further personal development. Ideally, this process is a positive experience, with an opportunity for a confidential and open dialogue, that will lead to appropriate action-planning for both you and your line-manager. These tips are designed to help you to get the most from the personal development and review system.

1  **Work through the documentation provided by your college.** This should give you a series of proformas or headings under which you look back at what you have achieved since your last review, plus any problems or barriers that you encountered. It will probably ask you in some form or other to self-evaluate your performance, both as a lecturer and as a colleague. It should also encourage you to reflect on the performance of your line manager. Focus on your own activities and on things which are directly relevant to the effectiveness and efficiency of your work. Do not dwell too much at this stage on broader issues of college policy (where **is** that network they promised two years ago?) or on the action (or inaction) of third parties.

2  **Agree the agenda for the review**. You and your line manager (who will normally be your reviewer) should discuss the nature of evidence you will be examining during your review including, where relevant, the outcomes of observations made of your teaching. Try to ensure that your reviewer allocates ample time to your review, and that the venue agreed will be private and interruption free.

3   **Use the review process positively.** Contribute assertively to the discussion by stressing what you want to get out of the review. Prepare a shopping list of what you would like to be the agreed outcomes, but be prepared to negotiate this. Clearly identify any new areas of work in which you would like to be involved. Be prepared to talk positively about any professional support, resources and development you will need in order to do your job more effectively and efficiently.

4   **A review of your past performance need not be a negative or unproductive activity**. Avoid seeing your review as raking over old ground or digging up past errors and mistakes. Use it as a chance to reflect and to learn from what went wrong or did not work. Do not use this part of your review to criticize other colleagues or to dwell on things which you (or your manager) have little control over (particularly a lack of resources).

5   **Remember that it is *your* review**. Do not allow it to become a one-way process, with your reviewer doing most of the talking. Use it as a proactive opportunity to affect your own working life. See your review as the most appropriate occasion to renegotiate your job description and make it more interesting or rewarding. If you regard the staff review process as a 'tokenistic' activity in which your manager is simply going through the motions, then that is what it is likely to become.

6   **Bring evidence of your achievements to the review.** For example, you might bring along student feedback data; print-outs of your students' achievements; examples of your effective organizational and administrative skills; and letters and memos from internal and external colleagues who have acknowledged your efforts. You can also tell your reviewer about examples of your dealing with problems; your contributions to strategic decisions; your promotion of the effective work and reputation of your college. As well as 'blowing your own trumpet', such evidence will most likely fill in the gaps in your reviewer's own knowledge about you, your strengths and your contribution.

7   **Use a part of your review to discuss local and college-wide issues that concern you.** These might include equal opportunity matters, health and safety issues, or your concerns about teaching, learning and assessment. The review process provides a rare chance for you to have the undivided attention of your line manager.

8   **Use your review as an opportunity to discuss your needs and wants.** You may be able to negotiate time or resources for professional training of various kinds. You might wish to gain approval for your participation in local or national activities relevant to your work. Remember that

professional development need not involve high expenditure. Opportunities exist for you to undertake personal development through work-shadowing, self-instruction and the use of staff development resource materials without large outlays of cash.

9　**Finish the review with an agreement as to what will happen next.** Normally this will involve a confidential written record of the review, together with an agreed action plan that includes deadlines and responsibilities for both you and your line manager. Make sure that you know who is doing what before the end of the meeting. Make notes in your diary so you can follow up agreed actions in due course. Contact your reviewer if you do not feel an agreed activity has actually been set in action or had any outcome.

10　**Review the review process.** If you feel that you have been short-changed by your reviewer because you felt rushed, not listened to, or not taken seriously, say so and do not countersign the formal record of the review or action plan. If you are happy with the way things have been done, make this clear, too, so that your reviewer, in turn, can use your satisfaction as evidence in his or her own review.

# 43

# Working as a part-time lecturer

Many colleges rely on part-time staff to present a diversified population of academics, as well as to build into curriculum delivery strategies a degree of flexibility. These tips, hard won from the personal experience of one of the authors, aim to help part-time lecturers keep a level head while all around are losing theirs!

1   **Learn to live with uncertainty.** The advantage to the college of part-time staff is that you are flexible and cheap. In many colleges, you are likely to be asked to step in at short notice to fill gaps, and you are unlikely to know what is expected of you until the last minute. Accepting this and learning to work in a permanently changing context will make for an easier life, and will bring its own benefits to you in terms of variety.

2   **Develop a range of flexible activities.** Whatever your subject matter, it is usually possible to devise a series of tasks and exercises to give to students when you are called upon at short notice. Such tasks give you a breathing space in which to plan your programme of curriculum delivery more strategically.

3   **Find your way around the college systems.** You will probably have to find out for yourself how to get photocopying done, how to use internal and external communications systems, and what to do to get paid. Make a checklist of questions to ask on your first day, and keep pestering people until you get the answers you need to help you do a good job.

4   **Network with other part-timers.** These are the people who are likely to have a lot of the information you need, as very often they are in the same boat. They can also provide you with good support when the going gets tough.

5   **Find yourself a full-time mentor.** This may be the person that you report to, or it may be another full-time member of staff working in your area who will be able to keep you updated on important college information. Such a person can also act as your champion in meetings you cannot attend, and ensure that the part-time tutors' perspective does not get forgotten.

6   **Help colleagues keep in contact with you.** Make sure that your home phone, fax and e-mail details (if available) are listed, and if possible clearly displayed on a staffroom notice board so you can be contacted when needed urgently. Check internal post systems and pigeon holes regularly, and ask a colleague to post mail home to you over non-teaching periods. It is easy for part-timers to get missed out if they are difficult to contact.

7   **Fight for the right to file.** Everyone needs space to keep records. Store students' work and file teaching materials. Part-timers often consider themselves lucky to have access to a desk and part of a filing cabinet, but you should argue for what you need to help you to do your job well.

8   **Bring your own mug.** Tempers get heated when part-timers inadvertently use other people's kitchen equipment, especially if they leave it dirty. It is also a good idea to bring your own tea/coffee/milk and so on, unless you are able to buy into a collective tea fund that does not disadvantage people who are not there all the time. Encouraging you to look after such things may seem a little isolationist, but you may find you need to make an appropriate choice between collegiality and survival.

9   **Set reasonable boundaries.** Part-time lecturers often find themselves called upon to work almost full-time for significantly less money than their fully contracted peers. It is especially common for part-timers to be pressurized into coming in for meetings outside their normal hours. You will need to balance a natural desire to be helpful, flexible (and employable), while at the same time not allowing people to take advantage of you. You may also need to check what your contract may say about meetings.

10  **Let people know what else you do.** Many people work part-time because they have other work or responsibilities. Artists, for example, often teach part-time to support their studio work, and many part-timers have caring responsibilities or other jobs. By informing people about your other lives, you will help them not to make unreasonable demands in your non-contracted time.

# 44

# Making sense of your contract

Your contract of employment is likely to set in general terms your duties and working hours, salary and working conditions. It will also have clauses pertaining to conflict of interest, confidentiality and copyright restrictions on what you do. In practice, it allows management a great deal of freedom over how your services will be used. These tips are aimed towards helping you to resist some of the less reasonable demands that may be made of you.

1   **Check out what is required of you.** In most colleges, what is expected of a lecturer is laid out clearly in the job description provided at the time of appointment. The staff review process is an opportunity to update or renegotiate your job description. Use this information to help you to make sensible decisions about how best to meet your obligations under your contract.

2   **Marshall your arguments against excessive front-loading of teaching hours.** A 'baseline' annual workload in at least one UK further education college has been reported to be 960 hours, although elsewhere a local agreement has settled for a lower figure of 828 hours. Whatever the figure in your institution, management can direct you to teach to it as they think fit. Too many face-to-face teaching hours in the early part of the academic year can result in burnout. This is especially true for those new to teaching, who have also heavy preparation workloads. Collect, with your colleagues, your constructive suggestions about how you can best support the uneven contact hour requirements over the college year. Robustly defend your right not to be placed under excessive strain early on, while still being willing to be flexible to a reasonable extent.

3   **Argue that staff development is a professional duty, not a privilege.** If you have negotiated attendance at a staff development course which is a necessary part of your personal and professional training, resist firmly attempts to timetable you to teach on the occasions when the course is run. Argue against the wasting of college funds which would occur if you were to be prevented from taking full advantage of developmental activities.

4    **Argue that you teach best what you know best.** College lecturers are often disconcerted by being asked to teach material that is far removed from their areas of expertise. Everyone needs to progressively diverge and develop in their areas of teaching competence, but too much chopping and changing is counterproductive.

5    **Be flexible about your working practices.** Curriculum delivery mechanisms are evolving, and lecturers who become hidebound by traditional methods will find life uncomfortable. Lecturers need to be prepared to develop the skills involved in writing and supporting open, resource-based and computer-mediated learning, but it is essential that they receive proper training and support to enable them to do so.

6    **Make a case to be given the right tools for the job.** Life can be made very difficult for college lecturers who know they need specialist equipment, software or information technology, in order to teach their subject well, but cannot get it because funds are tight. You should resist attempts to 'make do' to an unreasonable extent, and use the college's own quality arguments in your defence when necessary.

7    **Keep student needs up front.** We are short-changing our students if we are ill-prepared, under-resourced and exhausted. Use the needs of students to reinforce your arguments for proper support. This is particularly important in an era of student charters and partnership agreements, where students have rightful expectations of proper standards.

8    **Take a fair share of non-teaching responsibilities.** For a college to run effectively, everyone needs to contribute to administration, curriculum design, extra-curricular activities and so on, within the scope of their other duties. Look at these areas of work not as an additional burden, but as a part of your own professional development, building variety into your workload. Avoid, however, being pressurized into letting these things interfere with your other contractual requirements.

9    **Keep good records of what you are doing.** This will make it easier for you to defend yourself against unfair demands being made on your time, and will help you to challenge unreasonable requests, in a calm and logical manner.

10   **Look to your long-term professional development.** Sometimes it is worth taking on extra professional duties, because this will lead to you gaining experience in an area that might be helpful to you in promotion, or securing a better job elsewhere in due course. You will need to weigh-up carefully to what extent stretching your capacity to work now will pay off later in terms of experience and expertise.

11 **Be a good colleague.** From time to time, everyone needs to work considerably beyond their contractual obligations in order to support colleagues who are struggling for one reason or another. Be generous in your efforts where there is a short-term need; you never know when you will need such assistance yourself. However, do not let such a situation become a long-term problem; argue with your managers for effective alternative provision to be made.

12 **If the pressures become intolerable, seek help.** It will do you no good, nor the college, if you push yourself (or are pushed) beyond the limits of your own capabilities. If the workload pressed upon you is making you ill, tell your line manager, who has a duty to attempt to ameliorate the situation. Do not press on until the point of collapse, and do not assume that it is all your fault. Those putting excessive pressure on you must bear some responsibility.

# Chapter 7   Administrative and College-wide Responsibilities

Our final chapter continues with the theme of its predecessor – looking at ways of surviving in your professional life. This time we move to specific tactics that you can think about to make sure that you keep your head when all around you may be losing theirs.

We begin with some thoughts about meetings. Meetings are indeed necessary, but can easily get out of control in terms of the time and energy that they can take, and our suggestions are intended to counter such tendencies.

Next, we move to some suggestions about paperwork. Most colleagues we know claim that there has never been so much paperwork as there is now. The suggestions we offer here are based on our own battles to overcome mountains of paperwork, and we hope that among them you will find at least one or two ideas that you can put to use straightaway.

We continue with some suggestions on 'Working with administrative and support staff'. We are aware that the role of these staff within the sector is developing radically .They are no longer just employed to provide secretarial, clerical, library and technical support. They now may fulfil functions such as 'instructor' or 'learning adviser', and may be giving front-line support or initial assessment to students in learning centres, realistic work environments (eg, hairdressing salons) and workshops. It is therefore even more important to develop a cooperative and equitable working relationship with such staff. The amount of real help that such colleagues can give you should not be underestimated.

Our next set of suggestions moves to the external factors that can be involved in working with colleagues in higher education institutions with whom your own college may have formal or informal working relationships. We see collaboration with other institutions as not only desirable, but an essential survival basis for colleges.

We end this chapter, and indeed the whole book, with two sets of suggestions primarily about 'quality'. The first of these, 'Quality assurance and enhancement', gives specific suggestions about how quality enhancement can be built in to the everyday operation of colleges and the normal working lives of staff. The second set, 'Addressing the key issues', is based on key issues identified in England by the 1995–6 Report of the Quality Assessment Committee of the Further Education Funding Council (Circular 97/20, 1997). Among other things, this report identified the need to develop a 'more robust self-critical culture in colleges', and noted a lack of action plans for improved performance arising from quality assurance procedures. The Report argues that effective self-assessment is a matter for the whole community of each college, rather than for managers alone, and draws particular attention to the need to develop understandable measures of 'added value' and to exercise proper quality control over franchised provision, as well as to tackle the 'small but significant amount of poor teaching'. It has been argued that 'quality enhancement should be the only legitimate product of quality assurance systems'. Such issues have never been more important than they are now, with college funding dependent upon the outcomes of quality assurance procedures, and with staff development being increasingly focused towards quality enhancement. However, quality enhancement is not just in the interests of students attending our colleges, or those concerned with our colleges' overall performances, but is also central to a satisfying professional life for all who work in our colleges. This also means you, and we hope that our suggestions in this chapter (and in this book as a whole) will contribute towards increasing your own job satisfaction, self-esteem and professional performance.

# 45

# Coping with meetings

Committee work and meetings can take many different forms, ranging from course boards, exam boards and a host of other sorts of meetings. Most of the suggestions below are aimed at colleagues who are relatively new to participation in committee work, and who may find their first experiences of such work daunting, impenetrable or confusing.

1   **Decide whether you are sure you need to attend.** Life is too busy to attend irrelevant meetings. If you find that you do not participate at a meeting, you probably should not have gone to it.

2   **If chairing the meeting, ensure that the agenda has timings on it.** People need to be able to plan when to start the next thing they will do after your meeting, so a realistic finishing time should be worked out and published. Also, separate agenda items should be timed appropriately, so that all can be discussed adequately and fairly in the time available, and it can be clear to everyone when the time available for a particular item is about to be used up.

3   **Read your papers before you go.** It is also useful to find time before the meeting to read the paperwork – or at least to scan it – highlighting points where you may wish to make a contribution, and jotting down keywords which will help you to remember what you want to say.

4   **File your papers appropriately.** It helps you to keep on top of the paperwork and enables you to find what you need for the next meeting without stress.

5   **Read the last set(s) of minutes.** This is especially important if you are new to a group, as it helps you to get a feel for what is going on. It also helps you to feel clued-up, even if you have met the group several times before.

6    **Try to provide documentation in advance of the meeting.** Do this for key issues you wish to raise. What you have to say is likely to be taken more seriously if it is available on paper. It also means that there is less chance of your points being left until 'any other business', when they are more likely to be ignored.

7    **Try to submit any papers in advance rather than have them tabled at the meeting.** If people are presented with extensive reports at the meeting, such as with tables of figures, they will not give them as much attention as when they are able to go through them in detail in advance. Also, if quick decisions are needed on the basis of your papers, circulating them in advance helps to avoid the decisions being deferred on the request of some participants who may wish to spend more time with the papers.

8    **Make supporting papers short, precise and readable.** Try making an A4 summary if the information is detailed or contains support data or statistical information. Use bullet points rather than long sentences or paragraphs, and plenty of headings and subheadings to highlight the points you wish to make. Start each supporting paper with a short description of the issue or problem being addressed.

9    **List action points in supporting papers.** It helps considerably if it is clear at the meeting exactly what decisions are intended to be taken, and spelling these out boldly and concisely in committee papers can facilitate these decisions being addressed.

10   **Work out who is at the meeting, and make yourself a seating diagram so that you know who is saying what.** When names are not displayed on the table already, and if new to a committee, it can help you to pick up the threads of the different contexts and positions of contributors. Having people's names helps you to put names to faces in the future, and connecting what you have already heard about people to their behaviour and interests as seen at the meeting.

11   **Carefully note any action points down to you, and act on them.** You can wait to see the minutes to check what exactly your action points are, but make sure that you can be seen to have taken action before the next meeting. If you are unsure about what you are expected to do, or do not think it will be feasible, make sure that you speak about it at the time during the meeting, or approach the chair as soon as you see what the minutes have listed for you to do.

12    **If you are nervous about speaking, jot down your point or question before you speak.** This helps to boost your confidence, and means that if your nerve fails, you can still simply read out what you have written.

13    **Try to speak early in the meeting.** If you can find a reason to interject in the first 15 minutes, even though it might be to make a fairly minor point, you will feel more comfortable about speaking later. If you leave it too long, you might not feel brave enough to speak at all.

14    **When you wish to speak, catch the eye of the chair.** In some more formal meetings, the convention of 'speaking through the chair' means that it is thought to be bad form to speak unless authorized by the chair to do so.

15    **If you want to speak, and cannot catch the eye of the chair, raise your hand.** Normally a good chair is vigilant regarding who may wish to contribute, but no chair is infallible so you may need to make your gesture visible.

16    **Gauge the formality of the meeting.** Look and listen to those around you to discover whether first names are used, and whether conventions are treated casually, or whether this is a meeting in which you have to play by the rules. You will tell from the ways that people dress, the arrangement of furniture, and the status of the meeting, what is likely to be expected of you.

17    **Jot down your own notes at the meeting.** The minutes of a meeting may be minimal and focused on decisions rather than discussions, and may not cover all the detail that you may need to remember.

18    **Watch out for hidden agendas.** An astute meetings watcher may be able to discern all kinds of hidden currents and covert politics, which may influence outcomes more significantly than the actual contributions to the meeting. You may need to keep your eyes and ears open, particularly for subtle nuances.

19    **Be aware of the different roles adopted by participants at meetings.** Belbin (1993) identified a variety of different types of behaviour, including leaders, negotiators, teamworkers, implementers, completer-finishers, and shapers. Look out for who is taking which style of role, and use your observations on this to help you to interpret activities at the meeting.

20    **Don't let conflict in meetings rattle you.** Often you will find that postures are adopted and sabres are rattled, while the participants themselves often emerge from the meeting seemingly as the best of friends. Remember that behaviour in meetings can often be strategic and theatrical.

21  **If you get bored in meetings, use your own techniques to stay awake.** Give yourself permission to have 'out' thoughts, such as thinking about a cup of tea or about your holidays, for example by sketching your thoughts out. Then revert to note making on the serious ideas, having dealt with and dismissed the irrelevancies.

22  **If a meeting is irrelevant to you, consider leaving.** There is little point storming out, simply slip away quietly and with minimum disruption at a natural pause, so long as the conventions of the context do not make this seem hopelessly discourteous.

23  **Consider attending only parts of a meeting.** This is especially possible when there is timed business, and you can judge when to arrive and depart from the meeting according to when the items you need to attend for are timed. However, it is a fair assumption to expect most timed business to overrun.

24  **If you are asked to do the minutes of a meeting, or to chair a meeting, find out how to do it well.** There is not space in this book to go into full detail, but the difference between a good minute-taker or chair and a poor one is often about whether the people involved understand their roles and have had relevant training about how best to approach the roles.

25  **Learn the jargon of meetings.** You will need to be able to distinguish between a vote that is passed *'nem con'*, that is without anyone disagreeing, as compared to a vote passed unanimously, that is with everyone voting (no abstentions) and everyone voting in favour.

26  **Don't be afraid to ask questions if you do not understand something.** People on the whole will be quite understanding of those new to the process. It is better to ask than to be left in the dark. At worst, it is better to risk looking silly for a few seconds than to remain in ignorance for a much longer time.

27  **Prepare your data carefully.** If, for example, at an exam board, you may be asked to defend marks given to a student against quite robust criticism. Be prepared to justify what you have done, using strong evidence whenever possible.

28  **Take along all the equipment you may need.** At exam boards it often helps to have a ruler so you can follow a student's progress along a line of tightly printed figures, and a calculator so you can quickly check data, calculate averages, or add up scores.

29  **Take all your relevant paperwork with you.** You are likely to need class lists, for example, at exam boards, together with exam regulations, papers, copies of coursework mark schemes, and so on. Do not be embarrassed by having insufficient material to answer searching questions.

30  **Don't be put off by challenges from those more senior than yourself.** Often, they do not have the local or in-depth knowledge of individual cases and circumstances that you do, so be prepared to argue your case on the basis of what you know.

# 46

# Coping with the paperwork

Information overload (seemingly encouraged by the availability of computers) is a fact of college life. Usually the information is one-way – onto your desk. This paperwork may also appear to be not directly related to your own course and student responsibilities. The following suggestions can help you to take care of this general paperwork.

1   **Perform a crude sorting task on the paperwork.** Most of the paperwork can be safely filed. Some requires action on your part, either in creating your own paperwork or as an item for action.

2   **Prioritize your responses.** Deal quickly with financial and budget-related paperwork. Student records and assessment returns can have funding implications so should be dealt with as soon as possible.

3   **Employ time-management techniques**. Speed reading, scanning and review techniques are useful for dealing with copious paperwork. Setting aside a time each day to attack the paperwork can also help.

4   **Use your secretarial/clerical support staff.** Their job roles make them likely to be better able than you to efficiently process standard paperwork. They will be aware of any college protocols about official stationery, house styles, etc. There is also, because of quality monitoring and a growing interest in litigation, likely to be a requirement that all external and student (or student's sponsor) communications be centrally generated and a file-copy held.

5   **Use your photocopier.** Important but straightforward replies can be scribbled on the original, copied and returned.

6    **Keep files, not piles.** Handle each piece of paper as few times as possible. Try to avoid the situation of repeatedly sifting through piles of papers, looking for the particular documents you need. Equally, piles seem to 'lose' the document you want. If you think how long you have spent on occasions looking for a particular piece of paper, you will know in your heart that spending just some of that time organizing a good filing system would have been well worthwhile.

7    **Learn to love your wastepaper bin and shredder.** How often have you kept something to read later, knowing full well that you will never actually look at it again – except to remind yourself that you did not want to look at it? Allow a decent period of time to elapse and then feel free to 'weed' the files.

8    **Label your paperwork with Post-its.** These stand out easily from the papers themselves, and you can write short messages on them to remind you exactly what you are going to do with each of the papers, and save you having to read them all again trying to work this out again. You can make your own colour codes with the Post-its, maybe to remind you of the 'urgent', or the 'important' as opposed to the 'routine'.

9    **Use plastic wallets.** These are invaluable for making sure that all the papers that need to be kept together stay together. How often have you spent ages searching for that last sheet which has somehow escaped from a set of papers – or (worse) the first sheet?

10   **Get yourself a nine-part organizer.** These are indexed filing wallets, which contain nine sections, and are invaluable for collecting together the sets of papers which you are going to use in the immediate future. For example, one of these can contain the paperwork for each of the meetings you have in the next week or so, and it is much handier to just have to pick up one item to carry around with you rather than search for each meeting's paperwork in turn.

11   **Use alternatives to paper.** Would a telephone call be a sufficient response? Can you use e-mail? Electronic communication is quicker, less protocol bound, avoids paper and saves photocopy costs. Electronic scanners can be used to record incoming paperwork, then file and process the information contained. (The original paperwork can also be destroyed.)

12   **Save paper**. Use notice boards for things you want everyone in your department or section to see. For non-urgent dissemination, circulate a single copy of a document with a 'pass on to...' list, rather than sending everyone a copy – people who want their own copy can spend their own time making one. Make sure that the single copy is destined to end up in a sensible place at the end of its circulation, either back to you, or preferably in the departmental office for filing there.

13   **Take your paperwork with you.** Paperwork can often be done in odd moments between other tasks, and if you have it with you it is possible to make good use of such opportunities. But do not carry too much around with you; do not carry home more than you could reasonably expect to be able to do overnight or over a weekend. How often have you only had time to look at a fraction of the pile you carried home?

14   **Pass things on.** It is too easy to simply file (or junk) things that are not actually relevant to us. Keep in mind that they may be of use to a colleague. Put such things straight into the internal mail system, with a Post-it saying who they are for, from whom, and the date, and a cryptic message such as 'for inf.', or 'thought you'd like this', and so on.

15   **Keep *your* paperwork output to a minimum.** You will earn the gratitude of your colleagues if you do not add to the pile in their in-tray: use e-mail or the telephone. Keep any written work short and make it clear what you want them to do with it.

# 47

# Working with administrative and support staff

In an ideal world, we would not be differentiating between any of the people who contribute to the running of a college on any basis founded upon job title or job description. Those colleges which have abandoned such differentiation deserve high praise. However, it is still common to think of distinctions between staff who mainly teach, and those who mainly do other things. Therefore, in this set of suggestions we have reluctantly retained such distinctions, while at the same time offering advice that we hope will help to blur or remove such differentiation.

1   **Never neglect the courtesies.** Individual support staff sometimes over-inflate their importance and may seem to you to be overly bureaucratic or inflexible. Nevertheless, you will find it useful to gain their respect and cooperation. Ask, rather than instruct, and offer genuine thanks for the work done.

2   **Get feedback from support staff on the way you work with them.** Try asking support staff for feedback on your working relationship with them. Get them to say what actions you can take are helpful to them and what causes them concern. Apart from improving the effectiveness of the relationship, it can help you with your own self-evaluation of your performance.

3   **If you line manage any support staff, encourage them to network with other support staff.** This could be within your own college, regionally or nationally. Support networks exist for library, audio visual and specific areas of technical expertise. Remember their own professional updating and exposure to 'best practice' is as important as your own.

4    **Don't expect disorganization on your part to constitute an emergency on theirs.** Try to give fair notice for tasks you want them to do. Provide a clear statement of what you need doing. Check they understand and that the task is achievable in the time you have given.

5    **Help them to get credit for what they do.** Praise is always a great motivater, but do not just keep it private. If their contribution has been particularly good or critical, give them public acknowledgement and credit. If the particular member of staff is working towards a professional qualification or NVQ, such public backing can be used by them as portfolio evidence.

6    **Describe the precise nature and the priority of each task you ask them to do.** Photocopying and typing requests can often be accompanied by a pre-printed request proforma. Sometimes, where there are cost implications, you will need a budget code and the signature of the budget holder. Let them advise you, too, as they will be able to bring their experience to bear on the best way to do the job.

7    **Treat your support staff as equal partners.** If there are cultural or status barriers between academic and non-academic staff, do what you can to break them down. Remember that effective teamwork includes everyone, regardless of job description or remuneration levels.

8    **Help them to do a decent job.** Give them all the information and paperwork they need. Help them by providing full addresses, references or other data. The art of effective delegation is to give people responsibility for what they do, but also to provide support and inspiration to help them do tasks well.

9    **Use their strengths.** For example, they may be far better keyboard operators or video technicians than you. Find out what they are best at, and play to their strengths, as well as helping them to develop new areas of competence.

10   **Include them in social and morale-building events.** It is easy to forget that achievements and successes are usually the result of team effort. Such events do not always have to be expensive, externally facilitated away-days. Home-produced activities can often help a group to meld as well as anything more elaborate.

# 48

# Working with higher education

Collaborations, links and franchising arrangements between universities and further education colleges are increasingly important to both sectors, and even more so to the many students who move from one sector to the other. The suggestions below are intended to alert you to some of the principal issues to address to ensure that collaborations are fruitful and successful.

1   **Recognize that (at least in the UK) higher education and further education now have two very different cultures**. Bocock and Scott (1995) have clearly shown the emergence of two distinct cultures that increasingly distinguish UK further education from higher education. They characterize the very different experiences of further education students studying in higher education institutions (and vice versa), including the modes and methods of lecturers' support. You should not be surprised to find a distinctly vocational and anti-academic culture in a typical further education institution. At the same time, further education institutions may well be able to offer more individual support to students, and cater more flexibly for their individual course requirements, than can their higher education counterparts.

2   **Recognize each other's strengths and weaknesses.** Higher education institutions have better funding and library resources than their further education associates, but further education colleges often are stronger on dealing with students as individuals, and at providing detailed and personalized feedback on assessed work. Do not be surprised if your organization appears the more advanced in the use of flexible learning or the accreditation of prior learning.

3   **Be alert to the inclination of higher education to dominate the relationship**. Because higher education institutions are generally more generously funded and persevere with traditional notions of academic excellence, you may well find yourself being told to use a particular teaching and assessment method, or an array of resources. Your students are likely to be with you because your institution meets their needs, in preference to the higher education equivalent.

4    **Don't allow yourself to be intimidated by your higher education associates.** It may feel as if the staff in your partner institution are much better informed and qualified than you and your colleagues, but further education colleges have a great deal to be proud of, and can build up strengths in research and international links to match those in higher education.

5    **Find out about the formal agreement your further education institution will have with the higher education one, particularly concerning finances.** Partnerships between further education and higher education institutions only work when everyone concerned is entirely clear about *how* the arrangements are operated. Problems arise when there is lack of clarification about who is responsible for what, and when lines of communication are unclear or non-existent.

6    **Learn about your partner institution's processes and procedures.** It is essential that you are given all relevant course documentation, procedures, manuals and other paperwork. Some higher education procedures and protocols may seem impenetrable, so it is good idea for you to find a mentor or colleague from the higher education sector who can guide you gently through the more arcane and Byzantine elements of their rules and regulations.

7    **Help your higher education institution to learn about you.** Certainly let them have access to your documentation. More importantly, insist that they visit your organization and see at first hand your students, facilities and teaching–learning practices. Hopefully they will not then make artificial assumptions that you can do things the same way as them, or that your systems can readily be subsumed into theirs without loss of quality.

8    **Get and provide glossaries for each other's specialist terms and acronyms.** We often bandy about terms that are so familiar to us that we forget that others might regard them as a different language. Academics are infamous for developing TLAs (Three Letter Acronyms), and both sides need to make it as easy as possible for staff and students to learn each other's jargon.

9    **Keep in mind that higher education institutions are often working with significantly larger numbers of students than you are.** Some of the activities you propose with relatively small student groups in further education may be impossible to organize and monitor in higher education.

10   **Continually look for ways in which you can fruitfully collaborate with your higher education partners.** Can you, for example, undertake joint research, organize joint fieldwork for your students, look for joint bidding opportunities for external projects? Can you run collaborative open conferences, or open training events?

11   **Look for opportunities to make good use of each other's resources.** For example, it is likely that the higher education institution will have greater library and recreational facilities than your college that your students can use, even if you are charged for the privilege. They, meanwhile, may be keen to access your writing and numeracy development materials.

12   **Investigate joint staff training.** Your higher education partner may be happy for staff from your college to attend their staff development activities at little or no cost (where staff belong to institutions with a franchise arrangement), and both can learn a great deal from low-cost solutions such as work shadowing. It often helps for further education staff to shadow teaching by higher education colleagues before they start delivering a course themselves.

13   **Aim to have identified senior members of the higher education institution to smooth the way for your activities.** If this is delegated to a person at too junior a level in the higher education institution, they may not have sufficient clout with senior management to ensure that problems are solved and red tape is cut through. Equally, higher education academics can be as uncertain about their own institution's workings as you. Include, if you can, a senior administrative officer in your list of 'tame' contacts.

14   **Consider co-teaching with some of your higher education colleagues.** This is an excellent way for staff from different types of institutions to learn about each other's work contexts and to share each other's problems.

15   **Work closely with your higher education partner's educational liaison advisers, if they exist.** Usually higher education institutions will have a vested interest in helping further education students to move into their local higher education institution and will offer guidance and support within your college.

16   **Keep in mind your original reasons for collaboration with higher education.** It is possible to lose sight of the potential benefits of collaboration in the midst of all the organizational hassles it sometimes takes to make the collaboration work.

# 49

# Quality assurance and enhancement

Colleges are ultimately responsible for their own destinies and their continued survival depends on quality management. They need to ensure that all their processes and procedures are being carried out efficiently and effectively by their staff. For this reason, you will be expected to contribute to an *audit* of your team's activities so that the college has a clear basis for decision making. Equally, you will need (in your course team) to *assess* the quality of your teaching provision, and devise ways to *enhance* the quality of all your activities. These tips are designed to trigger your thinking about the quality assurance process.

1   **Start from where you are.** You need to collect the baseline data that exist about your college, so that you can map out the territory. UK colleges are now obliged by their Funding Council to have a mission statement, three-year strategic plan and annual objectives. These make an excellent starting point for your activity.

2   **Check out the external requirements for quality monitoring**. Colleges working under the UK's Further Education Funding Council (FEFC) will be subject to periodic inspection against extensive criteria and requirements. Equally, UK institutions receiving funding for higher education courses will need to satisfy the requirements of the Quality Assurrance Agency acting for the Higher Education Funding Councils for England, Scotland and Wales. Your college will also be required to take account of the quality requirements and reporting procedures, both of professional bodies and of examining and verifying agencies, for specific courses in its portfolio.

3   **Check out the internal requirements for quality monitoring.** Most colleges operate a range of internal checks and controls. These usually include student exit questionnaires, student satisfaction surveys, course reviews, course or service quality statements and monitoring.

4   **The increasingly common practice of self-assessment works on the assumption that the college's quality assurance processes are reliable and verifiable.** You, and your colleagues, will need to collect all the data to demonstrate that you are either meeting the prescribed criteria and standards, or that you are undertaking necessary corrective actions in areas of identified weakness.

5   **Look for opportunities for joint review where possible.** If you are in a team preparing for a course validation, be sure that your team correctly identifies all the stakeholders who will have a requirement to review your proposals. These might include your associated higher education institution, examining and validating bodies (such as EdExcel in the UK) and your college's own verification panel. Avoid 'quality fatigue' with you and your colleagues facing different reviews for different stakeholders.

6   **Find out what your students think.** Use a range of methods to elucidate students' views on the quality of their educational experience at your college. Be sensitive to the fact that no one likes to be continually asked to fill in questionnaires. If there are cross-college surveys, piggyback your particular requirements onto them. Sometimes you really need quality data rather than the 'tick-boxes' typical of surveys. Try getting volunteer students to participate in what market researchers call focus groups. Also consider doing some semi-structured interviewing with students, either on a one-to-one basis, or as a class activity. In these latter cases ensure you protect your students' anonymity and make it clear to them that any data used will not be attributable to them.

7   **Invest in expertise in designing student feedback instruments.** Questionnaire design, and market research generally, requires specialist skills if reliable and useful data are to be obtained. Use the expertise of colleagues who are comfortable with the appropriate research methodologies.

8   **Find out what your external stakeholders think.** Where practical, consult local employers, parents and others who sponsor your students. They can comment on matters, such as how well your college is doing in preparing students for employment or for higher education courses. As with student surveys, the standard questionnaire is probably not the best way of getting the sorts of information that will be most useful to you. Consider setting up, for instance, an employers' forum or focus group.

9   **Don't be dazzled by the statistics.** Once you have the data from your survey, there is the problem of interpretation. People tend to be beguiled by statistics into making overly simplistic, causal inferences from the data.

Use the best professional expertise available – your college is likely to have such people in their administrative sections of marketing or information services.

10   **Consider making quality standards explicit**. Many colleges have student charters and partnership agreements. Such documents set out for stakeholders what they can expect from the college and their rights and responsibilities, although legal concerns might make the commitments rather modest. The best contribution you can make is promoting the use of specific quality standards for the provision in which you are involved.

11   **Regard quality assurance as a process of continuous improvement, not a series of events**. You should see your contribution as part of a whole college, on-going quality focus. Quality assurance is not merely a paper activity for course validations or college inspections.

12   **Design quality review into the curriculum development process**. When designing new courses, or updating existing ones, make it a priority to decide how you will measure success and build in continuous improvement. Look at ways of piloting elements of new courses within existing ones, so that seemingly good ideas that do not work in practice can be remedied at an early stage.

13   **Use course management committees and course reviews to identify quality issues.** Documentation from such meetings can be used as evidence elsewhere in the quality process. This means that you can pick up a general quality issue quickly, and act upon it.

14   **Don't leave quality reviews to the last minute.** Ensure that you and your course team keep good records that track processes and provide monitoring data. This should be an on-going process. It is not just good housekeeping: getting the data together for quality review of all kinds is easier if good systems are in place already.

15   **Close the quality 'loop'.** Use all the data you assemble to help you enhance the quality of your course provision. For example, look immediately at ways of remedying the deficiencies identified from students' evaluations so that they do not reappear on the next set of evaluation surveys. Similarly, ensure that comments of external moderators and examiners are taken into action plans. Where problems identified are of a general resourcing origin or outside your control, inform senior management and those in the college who need to address the problem themselves. Ensure that any action (or inaction) on their part is fully recorded.

# 50

# Addressing the key issues

The following suggestions are derived from the main issues facing the further education sector as identified in the Further Education Funding Council's 'Report of the Quality Assessment Committee' published in 1997 as Circular 97/20. The Report divides its recommendations into four sections: management and resources; staffing; teaching and standards; quality assurance, and suggests who should take responsibility for addressing each of the issues identified. The issues are far from being specifically associated with the United Kingdom, and we end this book by using the needs identified in the Report as a summary agenda for development of further and continuing education. Many of the sets of suggestions provided in this book address the issues summarized below, and our primary intention below is to present all of the main issues together, with an indication of who may be expected to take a lead in tackling each issue.

## Management and resources

1   **Reflect on how best to achieve greater efficiency while maintaining standards.** College managers need to face up to the reality of having to reduce guided learning hours by looking at a variety of responses. These may include increasing class sizes, or relying more heavily on independent student learning.

2   **Work out how best to meet growth targets.** College managers, employers and others participating in training provision (such as the Training and Enterprise Councils in the UK) need to explore carefully how growth targets may best be met, for example, by developing a more diverse curriculum, a wider range of delivery methods, and by using an increased range of sources of funding.

3   **Improve college management information systems.** College managers and funding agencies need to support the development of systems that will effectively meet the requirements of managers, course teams and staff, as well as the self-assessment quality assurance frameworks being implemented.

4　**Strive to ensure that adequate funding is made available for capital equipment and major building projects.** Many readers of this book will feel somewhat powerless regarding this issue, with responsibility for financing such developments largely resting with government and funding bodies. However, it is important that everyone involved has an opportunity to participate in working out how best accommodation and capital needs should be prioritized. All stakeholders should seek opportunities to persuade college management, when necessary, to go elsewhere for sponsorship or other support for the equipment or accommodation that is necessary.

5　**Improve the provision of relevant learning materials and specialist equipment.** This is particularly needed to help to guarantee that students have adequate opportunities to develop key information technology skills. Funding bodies, college governors and managers have the responsibility to ensure that the equipment and resources needed for effective student learning are provided.

# Staffing

6　**Improve staff morale.** Most people working in further education have suffered a loss of morale in the face of rapid change, redundancies and longer working hours. Governors and college managers need to reverse this loss of morale, by ensuring that staff (part-time as well as full-time) benefit from relevant and continuing opportunities for personal and professional development. Staff morale may be best improved by the focus of college managers being seen to be the quality of student learning.

7　**Improve the management of part-time teachers.** This has been found to be an issue of increasing significance as the sector has continued to move towards a casual workforce, and college managers need to take positive steps towards ensuring that part-time staff have a satisfying and rewarding experience when working in the sector.

8　**Increase the abilities of people to manage change effectively.** Managers, governors and college staff all need to become better able to cope with rapid change effectively, and without undue stress. This should be an ongoing item for college management through its professional development and personnel functions. Government and funding agencies need to recognize the benefits of ensuring that there is a realistic balance between necessary change and productive stability.

9    **Ensure that teachers' commercial and industrial experience is relevant and up to date.** Governors and college managers need to achieve a comfortable balance between bringing in such experience by means of part-time teachers from commerce and industry, and at the same time giving full-time staff adequate opportunities to update their professional expertise.

# Teaching and standards

10   **Improve teaching standards in areas where deficiencies have been identified.** Governors, college managers and staff developers need to ensure that subject areas, where problems have been found, are targeted by relevant staff development focusing upon teaching, learning and assessment processes.

11   **Improve the levels of student attendance and retention.** Course teams, college managers and individuals need to play their parts in ensuring that retention rates for programmes are monitored carefully. Student attendance on college-based programmes needs to be addressed, and reasons for non-attendance need to be identified and followed up. The factors that lead to students dropping out need to be identified clearly, and used as the basis for targeted action to minimize dropout.

12   **Pay more attention to the development of students' key skills.** Course teams and individuals need to continue to focus on ways of improving students' information technology and numeracy skills, and to integrate such development into all aspects of the curriculum rather than attempt to address them separately.

# Quality assurance and quality enhancement

13   **A more honestly self-critical culture needs to be developed.** Responsibility for this lies with all stakeholders, including funding bodies and training providers, but particularly with college managers and course teams. This is particularly necessary as former inspection arrangements move towards procedures based on institutional self-assessment processes.

14   **College performance measures need to be more easily understood.** With the trend towards making colleges accountable in public ways, such as by publishing league tables of performance against specific criteria, there remains a need to ensure that the information published is valid and relevant. In particular, the most suitable measures are of factors contributing to the 'added value' which a college course brings to its students. Responsibility for identifying suitable measures normally resides with government and funding bodies, but it is valuable for college managers and staff to continue the search for the most appropriate measures.

15   **Franchised provision needs to be quality assured.** College managers, franchisers and franchisees all need to collaborate to ensure that where provision is franchised, particularly to distant or overseas institutions, that quality continues to be assured. This has implications for staff development, and for effective action by appropriate staff to ensure that quality assurance processes are well understood in franchised institutions.

16   **Staff development provision must tackle the small, but significant, amount of 'poor teaching' that has been identified in the sector.** This has implications for college managers, staff developers and training agencies supporting further education. Several sections of this book identify agendas which could be useful in rectifying problems of this sort.

# References and Further Reading

*(Note: many of the further reading references included mention the word 'university', but our selection from the literature lists sources that will be equally useful to staff in further and continuing education contexts.)*

Abramson, M, Bird, J and Stennett, A (eds) (1996) *Further and Higher Education Partnerships: the Future for Collaboration*, Open University Press, Buckingham.

Armstrong, S, Thompson, G and Brown, S (eds) (1997) *Facing Up to Radical Change in Universities and Colleges*, SEDA Series, Kogan Page, London.

Ashcroft, K and Foreman-Peck, L (1995) *The Lecturer's Guide to Quality and Standards in Colleges and Universities*, Falmer Press, London.

Ashcroft, K and Foreman-Peck, L (1994) *Managing Teaching and Learning in Further and Higher Education*, Falmer Press, London.

Barnett, L *et al.* (1996) *Technology in Teaching and Learning: A Guide for Academics*. Interactive Learning Centre, University of Southampton, Southampton.

Belbin, RM (1993) *Team Roles at Work*, Butterworth-Heinemann, London.

Bocock, J and Scott, P (1995) *Redrawing the Boundaries: Further/Higher Education Partnerships*, University of Leeds, Leeds.

Bourner, T and Race, P (1995) *How to Win as a Part-Time Student*, Kogan Page, London.

Brew, A (ed.) (1995) *Directions in Staff Development*, Open University Press, Buckingham.

Brown, S and Knight, P (1994) *Assessing Learners in Higher Education*, Kogan Page, London.

Brown, S, Rust, C and Gibbs, G (1994) *Strategies for Diversifying Assessment in Higher Education*, Oxford Centre for Staff and Learning Development, Oxford Brookes University, Oxford.

Brown, S and Smith, B (eds) (1996) *Resource-Based Learning*, SEDA Series, Kogan Page, London.

Chalmers, D and Fuller, M (1996) *Teaching for Learning at University*, Kogan Page, London.

Drew, S and Bingham, R (1997) *The Student Skills Guide* and *Student Skills: Tutor's Handbook*, Gower, Aldershot.

Earwaker, J (1992) *Helping and Supporting Students*, Open University Press, Buckingham.

Edwards, R (1997) *Changing Places? Flexibility, Lifelong Learning and a Learning Society*, Routledge, London.

FEDA (1997) *Learning Resources Centres: 7 Case-Studies in Proactive Planning and Management*, Further Education Development Agency, Blagdon.

FEFC (1996) *Inclusive Learning: Report of the Learning Difficulties and/or Disabilities Committee*, Further Education Funding Council and HMSO, London.

FEFC (1997) *Report of the Quality Assessment Committee for 1995–96: Circular 97/20*, Further Education Funding Council, Coventry.

FEFC (1997) *Learning Works: Widening Participation in Further Education*, Further Education Funding Council, Coventry.

Forsyth, IR, Jolliffe, A and Stevens, D (1995) *Planning a Course; Preparing a Course; Delivering a Course; Evaluating a Course* (The Complete Guide to Teaching a Course series), Kogan Page, London.

Freeman, R (1997) *Managing Open Systems*, Kogan Page, London.

Gibbs, G (1992) *Improving the Quality of Student Learning*, Technical and Educational Services, Bristol.

Gibbs, G (1994) *Improving Student Learning: Theory and Practice*, Oxford Centre for Staff and Learning Development, Oxford Brookes University, Oxford.

Harvey, L *et al.* (1997) *The Student Satisfaction Manual*, Open University Press, Buckingham.

Haselgrove, S (ed.) (1994) *The Student Experience*, Open University Press, Buckingham.

Huddlestone, P and Unwin, L (1997) *Teaching and Learning in Further Education*, Routledge, London.

Jarvis, P (1995) *Adult and Continuing Education: Theory and Practice*, 2nd edition, Routledge, London.

Jones, M, Siraj-Blatchford, J and Ashcroft, K (1997) *Researching into Student Learning and Support*, Kogan Page, London.

Knight, P (ed.) (1995) *Assessment for Learning in Higher Education*, SEDA Series, Kogan Page, London.

Leicester, M (1993) *Race for a Change in Continuing and Higher Education*, Open University Press, Buckingham.

McConnell, D (1994) *Implementing Computer-Supported Co-operative Learning*, Kogan Page, London.

Melton, R (1997) *Objectives, Competences and Learning Outcomes: Developing Instructional Materials in Open and Distance Learning*, Kogan Page, London.

Newble, D, and Cannon, R (1995) *A Handbook for Teachers in Universities and Colleges*, Kogan Page, London.

Peeke, G (1994) *Mission and Change: Institutional Mission and its Application to the Management of Higher and Further Education*, Open University Press, Buckingham.

Peelo, M (1994) *Helping Students with Study Problems*, Open University Press, Buckingham.

Race, P (1992) *500 Tips for Students*, Blackwell, Oxford.

Race, P (1994) *The Open Learning Handbook*, 2nd edition, Kogan Page, London.

Race, P (1996) *How to Win as an Open Learner*, 2nd edition, National Council for Educational Technology, Coventry.

Race, P and McDowell, S (1996) *500 Computing Tips for Teachers and Lecturers*, Kogan Page, London.

Saunders, D (ed.) (1994) *The Complete Student Handbook*, Blackwell, Oxford.

Silver, H and Silver, P (1997) *Students: Changing Roles, Changing Lives*, Open University Press, Buckingham.

Taylor, I (1997) *Developing Learning in Professional Education: Partnerships for Practice*, Open University Press, Buckingham.

Tight, M (1996) *Key Concepts in Adult Education and Training*, Routledge, London.

Webb, G (1996) *Understanding Staff Development*, Open University Press, Buckingham.

# Index